Thinking in Promises

Mark Burgess

Beijing · Cambridge · Farnham · Köln · Sebastopol · Tokyo

Thinking in Promises

by Mark Burgess

Copyright © 2015 Mark Burgess. All rights reserved.

Printed in the United States of America.

Published by O'Reilly Media, Inc., 1005 Gravenstein Highway North, Sebastopol, CA 95472.

O'Reilly books may be purchased for educational, business, or sales promotional use. Online editions are also available for most titles (*http://safaribooksonline.com*). For more information, contact our corporate/institutional sales department: 800-998-9938 or *corporate@oreilly.com*.

Editors: Mike Loukides and Brian Anderson	**Indexer:** Ellen Troutman-Zaig
Production Editor: Melanie Yarbrough	**Interior Designer:** Monica Kamsvaag
Copyeditor: Sonia Saruba	**Cover Designer:** Ellie Volkhausen
Proofreader: Charles Roumeliotis	**Illustrator:** Rebecca Demarest

June 2015:   First Edition

Revision History for the First Edition
2015-06-09:   First Release

See *http://oreilly.com/catalog/errata.csp?isbn=9781491917879* for release details.

978-1-491-91787-9

[LSI]

Contents

Foreword

Throughout much of human history, our technological achievement was driven by the quest for certainty and precision. Chaos in all its forms had to be defeated by the clockwork-like precision of the machines we built. We altered the course of flow of rivers. We achieved space flight. We created hierarchical societal structures with protocols and processes. But despite the mathematical precision, we never managed to achieve the robustness and efficiency of natural processes.

Our human intuition tells us that precise understanding of the underlying processes and consistency of their execution are key to well-functioning systems. This belief gives us a seemingly practical mental framework where all conditions affecting such systems are known and understood, or, at least, can be approximated or anticipated in some way. We further quantize the behaviors into sets of well-understood rules and actions and combine them in hierarchically organized global knowledge. A system of consistency hierarchies.

This approach led us to industrialization, but it also gave us an equivalent of industrialized micromanagement. Our control and automation systems turned into the equivalent of sequenced linear execution plans, where each step is a precise action—certain, predictable, and consistent. Any significant inconsistency leads to local and often cascading failure, at times, with global consequences—all with little or no ability to reconverge.

Our cultural preference for understanding the complete picture led us to the creation of control systems that function as large, centralized, all-knowing brains that make precise decisions based on assumptions of availability and consistency, resulting in actions that are elemental and imperative in nature—our intuitive strive to micromanage the reality. Such centralization, even if it's logical, leads to inadvertent limitations in scale. A centralized control brain, as large as it can be, still has finite processing capacity. A busy brain can't make decisions fast enough to carry out micromanaging actions in time. Latency of actions creates imprecision and inconsistency, often with unknown consequences.

In this book, Mark Burgess discusses a different philosophical approach to solving large-scale control problems that entirely eliminates the need for a big almighty brain and the very need for micromanagement. Instead, he focuses on breaking the system down into a large number of primitive functions, each fully autonomous, self-enforced, with the ability to deal with imprecision at the lowest level possible. Like in nature, these functions are not centrally orchestrated—they act like organisms that interact with each other in the form of promises, not subjected to absolute universal obligations, not requiring precise consistent knowledge.

—*Mike Dvorkin*
Distinguished Engineer at Cisco
June 2015

Letter to the Reader

Dear reader, this book is an introduction to what has come to be known as Promise Theory. It is addressed from a mostly nontechnical perspective. It is not a book that gives management advice, nor is it even about technical recipes; its goal is to help you to think without prejudice about cooperative systems of any kind.

We live in a marketing age where we believe that brands mean something, so today you'll read about Complexity Theory and Promise Theory and Theory of Constraints, and any number of other theories. Many believe that these ideas are all separate, competing sports teams, from which we are allowed to choose only one. Add to that Lean, Agile, Six Sigma, and any number of other management philosophies, and you are practically forced into primitive tribalism.

Promise Theory is not a management ideology; it is an engineering framework for coping with uncertainty in information systems. It is a set of principles, based on formal reasoning, without the over-constrained ideas of logic. Some people (not mathematicians) might call it mathematical because it has formal rule- or constraint-based approaches.[1] Others might say it is heuristic. These are subjective assessments, which are unimportant. In fact, Promise Theory has a lot in common with physics, being a mixture of both, but who cares about categories?

One of the reasons I started Promise Theory was to escape from the tyranny of fuzzy words that float around in management-speak. Words are verbose and often ambiguous, and people hear what they want to hear from them. Symbolic languages, like mathematics, express themselves simply and clearly, but many

---

1 In this book, I was instructed (on pain of retribution) to avoid anything that might resemble math. You have no idea the oppression that mathematicians face in society.

have been scared away from that precision by a poor experience with mathematics in school. For that reason, I started Promise Theory symbolically, but was quickly asked to go back to using words. That is what this book tries to do. Hopefully, having done a sufficient amount of symbolic homework, I can avoid some of the ambiguities that come from muddling words, but I am still wary. You should be too.

So why this word *promise?* Well, a promise is a word that everyone intuitively understands. It represents an intended outcome: something you might actually be able to get. This is pretty general, and indeed that is its value. For some, it is also confusing. The term does not have the arrogance or hubris of the more frequently used *guarantee*, and that is good. A broad swathe of society actually believes that the concept of a guarantee has merit (that merely promising without guarantee is somehow shirking responsibility). In fact, unless one has access to irresistable force and infinite speed, there are no guarantees.

Promise Theory has nothing to do with being nice. It is not about being moral. It is not about democracies rather than dictatorships. It is simply about realism, and attaching the responsibility for outcomes to the agencies that have the chance of being able to deliver. It doesn't tell you how to be immune to uncertainty, it just helps to clear away a veil of delusion, to see more clearly what kind of a mess you are in. The rest (getting yourself out of the mess) is up to good old human creativity (there you can hug as much as you like). What I will claim is that if, like me, you live in daily fear of appearing foolish by making unwarranted assumptions, then Promise Theory is the cold shower of common sense. It turns out to be a pragmatic way of coming to terms with the complexities of a world where you are not certain of having your way.[2]

Promise Theory came out of a need I had while trying to explain IT infrastructure and desired-state configuration in the early millennium years: studying how to manage human-computer systems. It became clear that computer science models, which were based on traditional logical reasoning, simply weren't able to describe computer behaviour, except in very isolated circumstances. Initially more mathematical, the ideas grew in scope and applicability, and over the

---

2 I have confirmed over the years that the wish for deterministic mastery over our world often works as a kind of homeopathy (trying to treat a malady with its own poisons). When we try to fight force with force (uncertainty with hopeful certainty), we end up in some kind of boxing match, often getting our proverbial rear-ends kicked. Smart martial artists try to use their opponents' real-time behaviours to their own advantage, and that is sort of the essence of Promise Theory. It's not what you *want* or *hope* for, but what you can *get* that matters. Pragmatism rules.

following decade began to be appreciated in a heuristic way, too. In a sense, Promise Theory is about one of the most general, yet contentious, issues of philosophy: causation. How things come to happen, and then remain, even in a noisy world.

As I was having my private eureka moment about promises in 2004, I was visited by Jan Bergstra, whose background was in logic and mathematical computer science. He also became interested in this issue from a background of rigorous logic and process algebra. Now my close friend and partner in what amounts to computer science heresy, Jan has been instrumental in boiling the Promise Theory story down to its essentials, and avoiding the pitfalls by which science becomes pseudoscience.

Amazingly, the idea of promises seems to have caught on in IT. However, for some, the idea has also become a manifesto for advocating ideas like decentralization and swarm intelligence. Although I am a big fan of those ideas, one should not think of Promise Theory as advocating them. Science does not advocate; it measures by theory and numbers, then tentatively concludes in context. An application of Promise Theory might lead to the conclusion that one design or another is better under particular circumstances, but never unilaterally.[3]

Looking at the philosophical and economic literature on promises, philosophers have muddled the idea of promises with the notions of obligation and morality. What caught our attention early on was that promises are an independent and simpler idea than obligations: something suitable for engineers.

The aim of this book, then, is to strip away the formalism—which I worked so hard to erect(!)—and introduce the pattern of thinking behind Promise Theory for engineers by words and pictures alone. This has been a difficult challenge because words alone lack the concision and clarity to make clear sense of a complex world. A more symbolic approach has been given in the book *Promise Theory: Principles and Applications* (CreateSpace), by myself and Jan Bergstra, and I recommend that book to clear up any questions you might have.

Writing a book for as general an audience as possible can easily result in the paradox of pleasing no one by trying to please all, so please forgive the compromises. I address the book to an audience of fellow technocrats. I hope, on the

---

3 It is perhaps natural that people gravitate to emergent phenomena and decentralization. These are interesting concepts, yet traditional computer science struggles to understand these issues with its deterministic "ballistic" reasoning.

other hand, that large parts of it can be read and understood by just about anyone in the modern world.

I am grateful to Michael Nygaard, Jeff Sussna, Paul Borrill, Mike Dvorkin, and, of course, Jan Bergstra for comments.

Promises and Impositions

Imagine a set of principles that could help you understand how parts combine to become a whole, and how each part sees the whole from its own perspective. If such principles were any good, it shouldn't matter whether we're talking about humans in a team, birds in a flock, computers in a data center, or cogs in a Swiss watch. A theory of cooperation ought to be pretty universal, so we could apply it to both technology and the workplace.

Such principles are the subject of Promise Theory. The goal of Promise Theory is to reveal the behaviour of a whole from the sum of its parts, taking the viewpoint of the parts rather than the whole. In other words, it is a bottom-up constructionist view of the world. You could describe it as a discipline for documenting system behaviours from the bottom up.[1]

Promise Engineering

The idea of using promises as an engineering concept came up in 2004, as I was looking for a model of distributed computing to describe CFEngine. The word *promise* seemed a good fit for what I needed: a kind of atom for intent that, when combined, could represent a maintainable policy. However, it quickly became clear (having opened Pandora's box on the idea) that there was something more general going on that needed to be understood about promises. Promises could also be an effective way of understanding a whole range of related issues about

---

1 There have been many theories of promises in the past, but here we refer to my work with collaborators. I described a more formal or mathematical account of Promise Theory in *Promise Theory: Principles and Applications*.

how parts operate as a whole, and it promised[2] something not previously taken seriously: a way to unify human and machine behaviours in a single description.

Unlike some other modelling methods, such as in business and computer science, Promise Theory is not a manifesto, nor is it a political statement or a philosophical agenda. The magic lies in the application of a simple set of principles. It is little more than a method of analysis and engineering for picking systems apart into their essential pieces and then putting them back together. Along the way, we find a method of representing and questioning the viability of our intended outcomes. For some people, this is what computer programming is about, and there have been many philosophies around this, like OO, SOA, UML, and so on. Many of these have failed because they set philosophical agendas ahead of understanding.

The purpose of this book is to ask what can an understanding in terms of promises tell us about cooperation in human-machine systems, organizations, and technology, and how can we apply that understanding to the real-life challenges of working together?

From Commands to Promises

The cultural norm, at least in Western society, is to plan out intended outcomes in terms of the commands or steps we believe we need to accomplish in order to get there. We then program this into methods, demanding milestones and deliverables to emphasize an imperative approach to thinking. This is because we think in stories, just as we relate stories through language. But stories are hard to assess. How do we know if a story succeeded in its intent?

If, on the other hand, we change focus away from the journey to think in terms of the destination, or desired outcome, assessment and success take on a whole new meaning.

Let's look at an example. Consider the following instructions for cleaning a public restroom:

Wash the floor with agent X.

Mop and brush the bowls.

Put towels in the dispenser.

---

2 Perhaps the most important thing about Promise Theory is that it drives people to the most terrible puns, without realizing that those puns say something involuntarily insightful, too.

Refill soap.

Do this every hour, on the hour.

Now let's convert this into a promise formulation:

I promise that the floor will be clean and dry after hourly checks.

I promise that the bowls will be clean and empty after hourly checks.

I promise that there will be clean towels in the dispenser after hourly checks.

I promise that there will be soap in the dispenser after hourly checks.

What's the point of this? Isn't the world about forces and pushing changes? That has been the received learning since the time of Newton, but it is an over-simplification, which is not accurate even in modern physics.

The first thing we notice is that some agent (a person or robot) has to make the promise, so we know who is the active agent, and that by making the promise, this agent is accepting the responsibility for it. The second thing we notice is a lack of motivation to make the promise. Cooperation usually involves dialogue and incentive. What is missing from these promises is a counterpart like: I promise to pay you if the bowls are clean. Thus a promise viewpoint leads to a question: how do we document incentives?

Why Is a Promise Better than a Command?

Why a promise? Why not an obligation, command, or requirement? In Promise Theory, these latter things are called impositions because they impose intentions onto others without an invitation.

Promises expose information that is relevant to an expected outcome more directly than impositions because they always focus on the point of causation: the agent that makes the promise and is responsible for keeping it.

Commands and other impositions fail us in two ways: they tell something how to behave instead of what we want (i.e., they document the process rather than the outcome), and they force you to follow an entire recipe of steps before you can even know what the intention was.

So, why is a promise better than a command? A promise expresses intent about the end point, or ultimate outcome, instead of indicating what to do at the starting point. Commands are made relative to where you happen to be at the moment they are issued, so their relevance is limited to a brief context. Promising the end state is independent of your current state of affairs (see Figure 1-1).

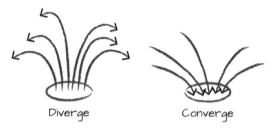

Diverge   Converge

Figure 1-1. A theme we'll revisit several times in the book is the divergence or convergence of time-lines. On the left, commands fan out into unpredictable outcomes from definite beginnings, and we go from a certain state to an uncertain one. On the right, promises converge towards a definite outcome from unpredictable beginnings, leading to improved certainty.

Promises also express intent from a viewpoint of maximum certainty. Promises apply to you (self) — the agent making them. By the definition of autonomy, that self is what every agent is guaranteed to have control over. Impositions or commands are something that apply to others (non-self). That, by definition, is what you don't control.

It's possible to promise something relative to a starting point: "I promise to stand on my head right now." "I will leave the house at 9:00 a.m." But promises represent ongoing, persistent states, where commands cannot. They describe continuity.[3]

Autonomy Leads to Greater Certainty

A promise is a claim made by someone or something about an intended outcome. It is not an insistence on action, or an attempted coercion. It is an expression of what I'll call *voluntary behaviour*. As we look at more examples, the sense in which I use the term voluntary should become clearer. Another word for the same thing would be *autonomous*.

An agent is autonomous if it controls its own destiny (i.e., outcomes are a result of its own directives, and no one else's). It is a "standalone" agent. By

---

3 You can always twist the usual meanings of command and promise to contradict these points, so we agree to use limited meanings that correspond to normal usage. In other words, this is not about the words, but about the ideas they usually represent. You can command yourself to empty the trash every Wednesday. Or you can promise someone that you are going to do a somersault right now. But it is hard to command yourself to do something persistently.

dividing the world up into autonomous parts, we get a head start on causality. When a change happens, we know that it happens within an autonomous region; it could not happen from the outside without explicitly promising to subordinate itself to an outside influence.

Note that a behaviour does not have to be explicitly intended for it to be intentional. It only needs to be something that *could* be intended or has the appearance of being intended.

The Observer Is Always Right

When we make a promise, we want to communicate to someone that they will be able to verify some intended outcome. Usually a promise is about an outcome that has yet to happen (e.g., "I promise to get you to the church on time for your wedding"). We can also promise things that have already happened, where it is the verification that has yet to happen (e.g., if your accounts department says, "I promise that I paid the bill on time"); the outcome has already happened, but the promisee has not yet verified the claim.

Why is this important? In fact, every possible observer, privy to relevant information, always gets to make an independent assessment of whether a promise was kept or not. The promisee might be the one especially affected by the promise outcome, but is not the only one who can form an opinion.

For example, suppose Alice promises Bob that she paid him some money. Bob was not there when she transferred the money to his account, so he cannot assess the promise until he checks his account. However, Carol heard the promise as a bystander, and she was present when Alice made the transfer. Thus, she can assess the promise as kept. Bob and Carol thus differ in their assessments because they each have access to different information.

This idea, that each autonomous agent has its own independent view, means that agents form expectations independently, too. This, in turn, allows them to make judgements without waiting to verify outcomes. This is how we use promises in tandem with trust. Every possible observer, with access to part of the information, can individually make an assessment, and given their different circumstances, might arrive at different conclusions.

This is a more reasonable version of the trite business aphorism that "the customer is always right." Each observer is entitled to his own viewpoint. A useful side effect of promises is that they lead to a process of documenting the conditions under which agents make decisions for later use.

Culture and Psychology

There are cultural or psychological reasons why promises are advantageous. In the imperative version of the restroom example, you felt good if you could write down an algorithm to bring about the desired end state, even once. Your algorithm might involve a checklist of items, like scrubbing bowls, using a special detergent, and so on. Writing down the steps feels pedagogical because it tells you *how*. It might be good for teaching someone how to keep a promise in the future, but it does not make clear what the final outcome should be, or whether there is more than one way to achieve the outcome. Thus, without a promise, one cannot assess the algorithm. With a promise, we can be clear about the desired end state, and also discuss alternative ways to bring it about.

The *how* is the designer part. What about the running and maintenance part of keeping a promise over time, and under difficult circumstances? In the world of information technology, design translates into "development" and maintenance translates into "operations," and understanding both together is often called DevOps.

If you imagine a cookbook, each page usually starts with a promise of what the outcome will look like (in the form of a seductive picture), and then includes a suggested recipe. It does not merely throw a recipe at you, forcing you through the steps to discover the outcome on trust. It sets your expectations first. In computing programming, and in management, we are not always so helpful.

Promises fit naturally with the idea of services.[4] Anyone who has worked in a service or support role will know that what you do is not the best guide to understanding: "Don't tell me what you are doing, tell me what you are trying to achieve!" What you are actually doing might not be at all related to what you are trying to achieve.

A simple expression of intent is what we call a *promise proposal*. By telling it like you mean it, it becomes a promise.

Nonlocality of Obligations

A major issue with impositions, especially "obligations," is that they don't reduce our uncertainty of a situation. They might actually increase it. Obligations

---

4 When I first proposed the concept in 2004, it was met with the response: this is just Service-Oriented Architecture (SOA). Although SOA is about promises, Promise Theory goes far beyond SOA's scope and goals.

quickly lead to conflicts because they span a region of our world about which we certainly have incomplete information.

Imagine two parents and a child. Mum and Dad impose their speech patterns on their innocent progeny as follows. Mum, who is American, tells the child, "You say tomaetoe," while English Dad says, "I say tomahtoe." Mum and Dad might not even be aware that they are telling the child different things, unless they actually promise to communicate and agree on a standard. So there is a conflict of interest.

But the situation is even worse than that. Because the source of intent is not the child, there is nothing the child can do to resolve the conflict; the problem lies outside of her domain of control: in Mum and Dad. Obligations actually increase our uncertainty about how the child will behave towards another agent.

The solution is to invoke the autonomy of all agents. Neither the child nor the Mum or Dad have to obey any commands or obligations. They are free to reject these, and choose or otherwise make up their own minds. Indeed, when we switch to that viewpoint, the child has to promise Mum or Dad what she intends to say. In fact, she is now in possession of the information and the control, and can promise to say one thing to Mum and another to Dad without any conflict at all.

Isn't That Quasi-Science?

Scientists (with the possible exception of certain social scientists) and engineers will bristle uncomfortably at the idea of mixing something so human, like a promise or intention, with something that seems objectively measurable, like outcomes in the real world. We are taught to exorcize all reference to humanity in natural science to make it as objective as possible. Part of the reason for this is that we have forgotten a lot of the philosophy of science that got us to the present day, so that we now believe that natural science is in some sense "objective" (more than just impartial).

In my book, *In Search of Certainty* (O'Reilly), I describe how the very hardest natural sciences have forced science to confront the issues of observer relativity (or what we might call *subjective issues*), in an unexpected twist of fate. As a physicist myself, it took me a while to accept that human issues really have to be represented in any study of technology, and that we can even do this without descending into talk about feelings, or moral outrage over privileged class systems, and so on.

The idea that a promise is more fundamental than a command or an obligation is not difficult to understand. It has to do with simple physics: promises are local, whereas obligations are distributed (nonlocal).

The goal of Promise Theory is to take change (dynamics) and intent (semantics) and combine these into a simple engineering methodology that recognizes the limitations of working with incomplete information. Who has access to what information?

When we describe some behaviour, what expectations do we have that it will persist over time and space? Is it a one-off change, like an explosion, or a lasting equilibrium, like a peace treaty?

Semantics and Dynamics

Dynamics are the aspects of a system that can be measured, like sizes, speeds, rates, and so on. Dynamical aspects of systems can be characterized objectively by numbers ("data"), and these numbers exist independently of an interpretation. In science, the words *mechanics* and *kinematics* are also used, but they are less familiar to a wide audience.

Semantics are about how we interpret something: what does it mean, what is its function, what significance do we attach to it? Semantics are subjective (i.e., in the eye of the beholder); hence one agent might assess a promise to be kept, while another assesses it to be not kept, based on the same dynamical data.

Is Promise Theory Really a Theory?

Like any scientific method, Promise Theory is not a solution to anything specific; it is a language of information to describe and discuss cooperative behaviour among different agents or actors. If you operate within the framework of its assumptions and idioms, it will help you frame assumptions and find possible solutions to problems where distributed information is involved.

Promise Theory is, if you like, an approach to modelling cooperative systems that allows you to ask: "How sure can we be that this will work?" and "At what rate?" You can begin to answer such questions only if some basic prerequisites can be promised by an agency involved in the possibly collaborative promise to "make it work."

Promise Theory is also a kind of *atomic theory*. It encourages us to break problems down into a table of elements (basic promises), from which any substantial outcome can be put together like a chemistry of intentions (once an intention about self is made public, it becomes a promise). SOA is an example of a promise-oriented model, based on web services and APIs, because it defines autonomous services (agents) with interfaces (APIs), each of which keeps well-documented promises.

The principles behind Promise Theory exist to maintain generality and to ensure that as few assumptions as possible are needed to predict an outcome. They also take care of the idea that every agent's worldview is incomplete (i.e., there are different viewpoints), limited by what different parties can see and know.

What is unusual about Promise Theory, compared to other scientific models, is that it models human intentions, whether they are expressed directly by a human or through a technological proxy, and it does this in a way that is completely impersonal. By combining Promise Theory with game theoretic models, we can also see how cooperation can ultimately have an economic explanation (sometimes referred to as *bounded rationality*). Why should I keep my promises? What will I get out of it?

The Main Concepts

We will refer to the following key concepts repeatedly:

Intention
> This is the subject of some kind of possible outcome. It is something that can be interpreted to have significance in a particular context. Any agent (person, object, or machine) can harbour intentions. An intention might be something like "be red" for a light, or "win the race" for a sports person.

Promise
> When an intention is publicly declared to an audience (called its *scope*) it then becomes a promise. Thus, a promise is a stated intention. In this book, I'll only talk about what are called promises of the first kind, which means promises about oneself. Another way of saying this is that we make a rule: no agent may make a promise on behalf of any other (see Figure 1-2).

Figure 1-2. A promise to give is drawn like Cupid's arrow...

Imposition

This is an attempt to induce cooperation in another agent (i.e., to implant an intention). It is complementary to the idea of a promise. Degrees of imposition include hints, advice, suggestions, requests, commands, and so on (see Figure 1-3).

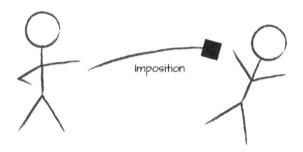

Figure 1-3. An imposition is drawn like a fist.

Obligation

An imposition that implies a cost or penalty for noncompliance. It is more aggressive than a mere imposition.

Assessment

A decision about whether a promise has been kept or not. Every agent makes its own assessment about promises it is aware of. Often, assessment involves the observation of other agents' behaviours.

There are other levels of interaction between agents. One could, for example speak of an attempt to force an agent to comply with an imposition, which might be termed an attack; however, we shall not discuss this further as it leads to discussions of morality, which we aim to avoid as far as possible.

Promises are more common than impositions and hence take precedence as the primary focus. Impositions generally work in a system of preexisting promises. Moreover, promises can often be posited to replace impositions with equivalent voluntary behaviours.

How Much Certainty Do You Need?

Promise Theory is still an area of research, so we shouldn't imagine it has an answer to everything. Moreover, it synthesizes ideas also discussed in other theories, like graph theory and relativity, so we should not imagine it is something completely new. It starts with a minimal set of assumptions, and then goes on to describe the combined effect of all the individual promises, from the viewpoint of the different parts of the whole, to form a network of cooperation. If you would like to understand it more deeply, I encourage you to study it in a more formal, mathematical language.

The word *promise* is one that seems familiar, and invites certain associations. In Promise Theory,[5] it has a specific and clear meaning. Others have taken the word for technical usage, too: futures and promises are discussed in concurrent programming. These also take the common word and attribute specialized meaning to it. We need to be careful not to project too many of our own imaginings into the specialized meanings.

As you read this book, you will find that Promise Theory says a lot of things that seem obvious. This is a good thing. After all, a theory that does not predict the obvious would not be a very good theory. Then there will be other conclusions that stretch your mind to think in unfamiliar ways, perhaps cutting through cultural prejudices to see more clearly. You might be disappointed that there there are no stunning revelations, or you might be wowed by things you have never realized before. It all depends on where you start your thought process. Whatever your experience, I hope this book will offer some insights about formulating and designing systems for cooperation.

---

5 Promise Theory, in the sense of this book, refers to a specific theory that emerged from my work around distributed computing. There are other theories about the meaning of promises in philosophy, which I promise to politely ignore throughout this book.

A Quick User Guide

Let's briefly sketch how to start thinking in promises, before delving into the details. It boils down to a few rules of thumb:

Identify the key players (agents of intent)

The first step in modelling is to identify the agencies that play roles within the scope of the problem you are addressing. An agent is any part of a system that can intend or promise something independently, even by proxy. Some agents will be people, others will be computers, policy documents, and so on—anything that can document intent regardless of its original source.

To get this part of the modelling right, we need to be careful not to confuse intentions with actions or messages. Actions may or may not be necessary to fulfill intentions. Maybe inaction is necessary!

Also, you shouldn't be squeamish about attributing promises to blunt instruments. We might be talking about the parts of a clock, or even an HTTP request, as agencies within a system. The motivations that play a role in making a bigger picture are not necessarily played out by humans in the end game.[6]

To be independent, an agent only needs to think differently or have a different perspective, access to different information, and so on. This is about the separation of concerns. If we want agents that reason differently to work together, they need to promise to behave in a mutually beneficial way. These agents can be humans (as in the business-IT bridge) or computers (as in a multitier server queue).

Deal with the uncertainties and obstacles

How likely is it that the agent will be able to keep the promise? In the real world there is no absolute certainty, so forget about that right now! Dealing with uncertainty is what science is really for, so roll up your sleeves and prepare to engineer your promises to make the best of what you have to work with. There are techniques for this.

---

6 All intentions originate with human observers if we trace them back far enough. But many day-to-day objects can be vehicles of those intentions, and therefore act as proxies. A cup is just a piece of ceramic; its intent to act as a cup is something a designer (acting on behalf of a user) decided. From a modelling perspective, that chain of provenance is not usually important, so we simply attach the promise to the inanimate cup. Now that it exists, that is the promise it makes to potential users.

The bottom line is that promises might or might not be kept (for a hundred different reasons). After all, they are only intentions, not irresistible forces.

Machines and people alike can break down and fail to keep a promise, so we need to model this. Each promise will have some kind of likelihood (perhaps even a formal probability) associated with it, based on our trust or belief in its future behaviour.[7]

Agents only keep promises about their own behaviour, however. If we try to make promises on others' behalf, they will most likely be rejected, impossible to implement, or the other agent might not even know about them. So it is a *pull* or *use what's promised* model of the world rather than a *push* or *try to impose on others* model. It assumes that agents only bend to external imposition if they want to (i.e., control cannot be pushed by force). That means we have to look more realistically upon illusions like forcible military command structures, and see them as cases where there is actually a consensus to voluntarily follow orders—even when these sometimes fail.

From requirements to promises (top-down to bottom-up)

Promise Theory focuses attention on the active agents for two reasons: first, because these are the ones that know most about their own ability to keep promises. Second, because the active agents are the atomic building blocks that can be added easily into any larger act of cooperation. Requirements get imposed top-down. Promises are kept bottom-up.

This is analogous to the insight made by atomic theory. Think of chemistry and the table of atomic elements. No one can invent a new element by imposing a requirement. Imagine designing a plane that requires a metal with twice the strength of steel but half the weight of aluminium. You can try writing to Santa Claus to get it for Christmas, but the laws of physics sort of get in the way. We can dream of things that are simply not possible, but if we look at what the world promises and try to build within that, instead of dreaming arbitrarily, we will make real progress. From the promised chemistry of the basic elements, we can build combinations of

---

7 The simplistic two-state model of faults, where manufacturers like to talk of all their 9s, the expressions Mean Time Before Failure (MTBF) and Mean Time To Repair (MTTR) are coined. These are probabilistic measures, so they have to be multiplied by the number of instances we have. In today's massive-scale environments, what used to be a small chance of failure or MTBF gets amplified into a large one. To counter this, we need speedy repair if we are going to keep our promises.

elements with new material properties, just by understanding how the individual types of atoms with their different properties (i.e., promises to behave) combine.

This is a bottom-up strategy. When you work from the top down, your whole viewpoint is nonlocal, or distributed. You are not thinking clearly about where information is located, and you might make assumptions that you have no right to make; for example, you might effectively make promises on behalf of agents you don't control.

On the other hand, when you work from the bottom up, you have no choice but to know where things are because you will need to document every assumption with an explicit promise. Thus, a promise approach forces a discipline.

Isn't this just an awkward way of talking about requirements? Not really. It is the opposite. A requirement is an obligation from a place of high-level generalization onto a place of more expert execution. There is an immediate information gap or disconnect between requirer and requiree. The important information about the likely outcome is at the wrong end of that gap. From a promise viewpoint, you force yourself to think from the point of execution and place yourself in the role of keeping the promise, confronting all the issues as they appear. It is much harder to make unwarranted assumptions when you do this.

Thinking in promises also makes you think about contingency plans. What if your first assumptions fail?

The promise position is an extreme position, one that you might object to on some grounds of convention. It is because it is an extreme position that it is useful. If we assume this, we can reconstruct any other shade of compliance with outside influence by documenting it as a promise. But once we've opened the door to doubt, there is no going back. That's why this is the only rational choice for building a theory that has any predictive power.

The goal in Promise Theory is thus to ensure that agents cooperate by making all the promises necessary to collectively succeed. A magical onlooker, with access to all the information, would be able to say that an entire cooperative operation could be seen as if it were a single organism making a single promise. How we coax the agents to make promises depends on what kinds of agents they are. If they are human, economic incentives are the generic answer. If the agents are programmable, then they need to be programmed to keep the promises. We call this *voluntary cooperation*. For humans, the economics are social, professional, and economic.

Is this crazy? Why not just force everyone to comply, like clockwork? Because that makes no sense. Even a computer follows instructions only because it was constructed voluntarily to do so. If we change that promise by pulling out its input wires, it no longer does. And, as for humans, cooperation is voluntary in the sense that it cannot be forced by an external agent without actually attacking the system to compromise its independence.

Deal with conflicts of intent

If all agents shared the same intentions, there would not be much need for promises. Everyone would get along and sing in perfect harmony, working towards a common purpose. The fact that the initial state of a system has unknown intentions and distributed information means that we have to set up things like agreements, where agents promise to behave in a certain way. This is what we call orchestration.

But what if promises in different locations affect a third party unwittingly? This happens quite a lot, as an emergent effect. In obligation theories (requirements, laws, and distributed permission models), the possibility for conflict is very high. Promise Theory is rather good at resolving conflicts because an agent can only conflict with itself, hence all the information to resolve the conflicts is located in the same place.

Just Make It Happen

Promise Theory seems upside down to some people. They want to think in terms of obligations. A should do B, C must do D, and so on. But apart from riling a human being's sense of dignity, that approach quickly leads to provable inconsistencies. The problem is that the source of any obligation (the obliger) is external to the agent that is being obliged. Thus if the agent is either unable or unwilling to cooperate (perhaps because it never received a message), the problem cannot be resolved without solving another distributed cooperation problem to figure out what went wrong! And so on, ad nauseum. (One begins to see the fallacy of trusting centralized push models and separate monitoring systems.)

Promise Theory assumes that an agent can only make promises about its own behaviour (because that is all it is in control of), and this cuts through the issues surrounding distribution of information, ensuring that both the information and resources needed to resolve any problem are local and available to the agent. In this way, an agent can autonomously repair a promise by taking responsibility. This is the meaning of agency.

An Exercise

Test yourself on your ability to think in terms of promises instead of desires, requirements, needs, and so on. Spend a whole day thinking about the promises made by people, places, processes, and things:

- To whom are the promises made?
- In what form are the promises made?
- Do they depend on something else to help them keep their promise?
- How do these things try to keep their promises?
- How do you assess their success?

Don't miss anything: from the bed you get out of (did it give you back pain?), to your morning exercise regimen (will it reduce fat?), the food you eat (is it fresh, tasty?), the people you work with (what are their roles?), the city you live in, all the way up to the toothbrush you end your day with.

If you can't see any promises, try asking yourself: what is the intended function? What is my relationship with these things? What value do I see in them? Finally, what additional interpretations do you add, which are not part of the promises around you? Does money mean lifestyle, recreation, savings for a rainy day?

At the end of your day, you will have a better understanding of what we call *semantics* and *intentionality* in the world, and you will be ready to apply that thinking to all kinds of situations.

2

With a License to Intend

Intentionality is that elusive quality that describes purpose. It is distinctly human judgement. When we intend something, it contributes meaning to our grand designs. We measure our lives by this sense of purpose. It is an intensely sensitive issue for us. Purpose is entirely in the eye of the beholder, and we are the beholders.

An Imposition Too Far

Throwing a ball to someone, without warning, is an imposition. There was no preplanned promise that advertised the intention up front; the ball was simply aimed and thrown. The imposition obviously does not imply an obligation to catch the ball. The imposee (catcher) might not be able to receive the imposition, or might be unwilling to receive it. Either way, the autonomy of the catcher is not compromised by the fact that the thrower attempts to impose upon it.

The thrower might view the purpose of the imposition as an act of kindness, for example, inviting someone to join in the fun. The recipient might simply be annoyed by the imposition, being uninterested in sport or busy with something else.

In the second part of Figure 2-1, the two players have promised to throw and catch, perhaps as part of the agreement to play a game. Was this a rule imposed on them? Perhaps, but in that case they accepted it and decided to promise compliance. If not, perhaps they made up the "rule" themselves. A rule is merely a seed for voluntary cooperation.

Figure 2-1. An imposition does not imply coercion. Autonomous agents still participate voluntarily. On the right, a lack of a promise to respond might be an unwillingness to respond or an inability to respond.

Reformulating Your World into Promises

Seeing the world through the lens of promises, instead of impositions, is a frame of mind, one that will allow you to see obvious strengths and weaknesses quickly when thinking about intended outcomes.

Promises are about signalling purpose through the language of intended outcomes. Western culture has come to use obligation and law as a primary point of view, rather than autonomous choice, which is more present in some Eastern cultures. There is a lawmaking culture that goes back at least as far as the Biblical story of Moses. Chances are, then, that you are not particularly used to thinking about everyday matters in terms of promises. It turns out, however, that they are absolutely everywhere.

Here are some examples of the kinds of statements we may refer to as promises:

- I promise you that I will walk the dog.
- I promise you that I fed your cat while you were away.
- We promise to accept cash payments.
- We promise to accept validated credit cards.
- I'll lock the door when I leave.
- I promise not to lock the door when I leave.
- We'll definitely wash our hands before touching the food.

These examples might be called something like *service promises*, as they are promises made by one agent about something potentially of value to another. We'll return to the idea of services promises often. They are all intended outcomes yet to be verified.

Proxies for Human Agency

Thanks to human ingenuity and propensity for transference (some might say anthropomorphism, if they can pronounce it), promises can be made by inanimate agents too. Inanimate objects frequently serve as proxies for human intent. Thus it is useful to extend the notion of promises to allow inanimate objects and other entities to make promises. Consider the following promises that might be made in the world of information technology:

- The Internet Service Provider promises to deliver broadband Internet for a fixed monthly payment.
- The security officer promises that the system will conform to security requirements.
- The support personnel promise to be available by pager 24 hours a day.
- Support staff promises to reply to queries within 24 hours.
- Road markings promise you that you may park in a space.

- An emergency exit sign promises you a way out.

These are straightforward promises that could be made more specific. The final promise could also be restated in more abstract terms, transferring the promise to an abstract entity, "the help desk":

- The company help desk promises to reply to service requests within 24 hours.
- The weather promises to be fine.

This latter example illustrates how we transfer the intentions of promises to entities that we consider to be responsible by association. It is a small step from this transference to a more general assignment of promises to individual components in a piece of technology. We abstract agency by progressive generalization:

- Martin on the front desk promised to give me a wake-up call at 7 a.m.
- The person on the front desk promised to give me a wake-up call at 7 a.m.
- The front desk promised to give me a wake-up call at 7 a.m.

Suddenly what started out as a named individual finds proxy in a piece of furniture.

In a similar way, we attach agency to all manner of tools, which may be considered to issue promises about their intended function:

- I am a doctor and I promise to try to heal you.
- I am a meat knife and promise to cut efficiently through meat.
- I am a logic gate and promise to transform a TRUE signal into a FALSE signal, and vice versa.
- I am a variable that promises to represent the value 17 of type integer.
- I am a command-line interpreter and promise to accept input and execute commands from the user.
- I am a router and promise to accept packets from a list of authorized IP addresses.

- I am a compliance monitor and promise to verify and automatically repair the state of the system based on this description of system configuration and policy.

- I am a high availability server, and I promise you service delivery with 99.9999% availability.

- I am an emergency fire service, and I promise to come to your rescue if you dial 911.

From these examples we see that the essence of promises is quite general. Indeed such promises are all around us in everyday life, both in mundane clothing as well as in technical disciplines. Statements about engineering specifications can also profitably be considered as promises, even though we might not ordinarily think of them in this way.

Practice reformulating your issues as promises.

What Are the Agencies of Promises?

Look around you and consider what things (effectively) make promises.

- A friend or colleague
- The organization you work for
- A road sign
- A pharmaceutical drug
- A table
- A nonstick pan
- A window
- A raincoat
- The floor
- The walls
- The book you are reading
- The power socket

What Issues Do We Make Promises About?

What might be the subject of a promise? Outcomes of different kinds:

- A function or service provided
- A value judgement (say about fitness for purpose)
- Access or permission to use something
- Behaviour (rules, laws)
- Timing
- Location
- Layout or configuration

What Things Can Be Promised?

Things that make sense to promise are things we know can be kept (i.e., brought to a certain state and maintained).

- States, arrangements, or configurations, like a layout
- Idempotent operations (things that happen once): delete a file, empty the trash
- Regular, steady state, or continuous change: constant speed
- An event that already happened

What Things Can't Be Promised?

We already said that the basic rule of autonomy is that an agent cannot make a promise about anyone or anything other than itself. This is a simple rule of thumb. If it did, another agent assessing the promise would be right to reject that promise as a breach of trust and devalue the promiser's reputation, as it is clear speculation.

For example, a manager might try to promise that her team will deliver a project by a deadline. If she is honest, she will make this conditional on the cooperation of the members of her team, otherwise this is effectively an imposition on her team (with or without their knowing). It might even be a lie or a deception (the dark side of promises). Without promises from each of her team members, she has no way of knowing that they will be able to deliver the project by the deadline. If this seems silly, please think again. The aim of science is for realism, not for unrealistic authority. Impositions do not bring certainty; promises that we trust are a kind of best guess.

Are there any other limitations?

Changes that are relative rather than absolute don't make much sense as promises—for example, turn left, turn upside down. Technically, these are imperatives, or nonidempotent commands. Each time we make the change, the outcome changes, so we can't make a promise about a final outcome. If we are talking about the action itself, how do we verify that it was kept? How many times should we turn? How often?

The truth is, anyone can promise anything at all, as in Monty Python's sketch "Stake Your Claim!", where contestants promise: "I claim that I can burrow through an elephant!" and "I claim that I wrote all of Shakespeare's plays, and my wife and I wrote his sonnets." These things are, formally, promises. However, they are obviously deceptions, or outright lies. If we lie and are found out, the value of our promises is reduced as a consequence.

The impartial thing to do would be to leave this as a matter for other agents to assess, but there are some basic things that nature itself promises, which allow us to draw upon a few rules of thumb.

A minimum requirement for a promise might be for there to exist some kind of causal connection between the promiser and the outcome of a promise in order to be able to keep it (i.e., in order for it to be a plausible promise).[1] So it would be fine to promise that you fed someone's cat, but less plausible to promise that you alone created the universe you were born into.

The Lifecycle of Promises

The promise lifecycle refers to the various states through which a promise passes, from proposal to the end (see Table 2-1). The lifecycle of a promise may

---

1 Statisticians these days are taught that causation is a dirty word because there was a time when it was common to confuse correlation with causation. Correlation is a mutual (bidirectional) property, with no arrow. Causation proper, on the other hand, refers to the perceived arrow of time, and basically says that if A precedes B, and there is an interaction between the two, then A might contribute to B, like a stepping stone. This is unproblematic.

now be viewed from either the perspective of the agent making the promise (Figure 2-2), or from the perspective of the promisee (Figure 2-3), or in fact any another agent that is external but in scope of the promise.

Table 2-1. The lifecycle of promises

Promise State	Description
proposed	A promise statement has been written down but not yet made.
issued	A promise has been published to everyone in its scope.
noticed	A published promise is noticed by an external agent.
unknown	The promise has been published, but its outcome is unknown.
kept	The promise is assessed to have been kept.
not kept	The promise is assessed to have been not kept.
broken	The promise is assessed to have been broken.
withdrawn	The promise is withdrawn by the promiser.
expired	The promise has passed some expiry date.
invalidated	The original assumptions allowing the promise to be kept have been invalidated by something beyond the promiser's control.
end	The time at which a promise ceases to exist.

Once a promise is broken or otherwise enters one of its end states (invalidated, expired, etc.), its lifecycle is ended, and further intentions about the subject must be described by new promises.

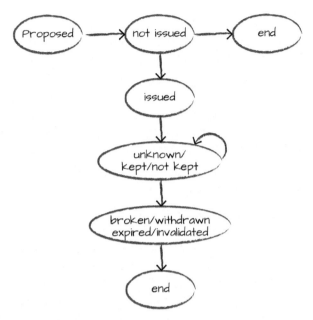

Figure 2-2. The promise lifecycle for a promiser.

From the perspective of the promisee, or other external agent in scope, we have a similar lifecycle, except that the promise is first noticed when published by the promiser (Figure 2-3).

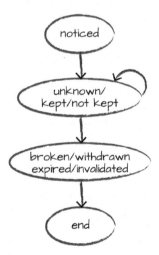

Figure 2-3. The promise lifecycle for a promisee.

Keeping Promises

What does it mean to keep a promise? What is the timeline? When is a promise kept? How many events need to occur? What needs to happen? What is the life-cycle of a promise? Probably it means that some essential state has changed or been preserved in an agent's world, or its state has been maintained or preserved. The configuration of the world measures the outcome of a promise. The result also has a value to the agent. These things are assessments to be made by any agent that knows about the promise. Agents can assess promises differently, each based on their own standards. What one agent considers as a promise kept might be rejected by another as inadequate.

Cooperation: The Polarity of Give and Take

When promises don't go in both directions, a cooperative relationship is in danger of falling apart and we should be suspicious. Why would one agent be interested in the other agent, if not mutual intent? This is a sign of potential instability. This seems initially trite and a human-only limitation, but even machinery works in this way. Physics itself has such mechanisms built into it.

In reality, promises and impositions are always seen from the subjective vantage point of one of the autonomous agents. There is not automatically any "God's-eye view" of what all agents know. We may call such a subjective view the "world" of the agent. In computer science, we would call this a distributed system. Promises have two polarities, with respect to this world: inwards or outwards from the agent.

- Promises and impositions to give something (outwards from an agent)

- Promises and impositions to receive something (inwards to an agent)

In the mathematical formulation of promises, we use positive and negative signs for these polarities, as if they were charges. It's easy to visualize the differences with examples:

- A (+) promise (to give) could be: "I promise you a rose garden," or "I promise email service on port 25."

- A (-) promise (to use/receive) could be: "I accept your offer of marriage," or "I accept your promise of data, and add you to my access control list."

- A (+) imposition (to give) could be: "You'd better give me your lunch money!" or "You'd better give me the address of this DNS domain!"

- A (-) imposition (to use/receive) could be: "Catch this!" or "Process this transaction!"

For every promise made to serve or provide something (call it X) by one agent in a supply chain, the next agent has to promise to use the result X in order to promise Y to the next agent, and so on. Someone has to receive or use the service (promises labelled "-") that is offered or given (promises labelled "+"). So there is a simple symmetry of intent, with polarity like a battery driving the activity in a system. Chains, however, are fragile: every agent is a single point of failure, so we try for short-tiered cooperatives. In truth, most organizations are not chains, but networks of promises.

If one agent promises to give something, this does not imply that the recipient agent promises to accept it, since that would violate the principle of autonomy. This also applies if an agent imposes on another agent, for example to give something (please contribute to our charity), or to receive something (you really must accept our charity). Neither of these need influence the agent on which one imposes these suggestions, but one can try nevertheless.

The plus-minus symmetry means that there are two viewpoints to every problem. You can practice flipping these viewpoints to better understand systems.

How Much Does a Promise Binding Count?

An author promises his editor to write 10 pages, and the editor promises to accept 5 pages. The probable outcome is that 5 pages will end up in print. Similarly, if the author promises to write 5 pages and the editor promises to print 10, the probable outcome is 5 pages, though it might be zero if there is an additional condition about all or nothing. If a personal computer has a gigabit network adapter, but the wall connection promises to deliver only 100 megabits, then the binding will be 100 megabits.

Promises and Trust Are Symbiotic

The usefulness of a promise is intimately connected with our *trust* in the agents making promises. Equivalently we can talk of the *belief* that promises are valid, in whatever meaning we choose to apply. In a world without trust, promises would be completely ineffective.

For some, this aspect of the world promise could be disconcerting. Particularly, those who are progeny of the so-called "exact sciences" are taught to describe the world in apparently objective terms, and the notion of something that involves human subjective appraisal feels intuitively wrong. However, the role of promises is to offer a framework for reducing the uncertainty about the outcome of certain events, not to offer guarantees or some insistence on determinism. In many ways, this is like the modern theories of the natural world where indeterminism is built in at a fundamental level, without sacrificing the ability to make predictions.

Promoting Certainty

Promises express outcomes, hopefully in a clear way. If promises are unclear, they have little value. The success of promises lies in being able to make assertions about the intent of a thing or a group of things.

The autonomy principle means that we always start with the independent objects and see how to bring them together. This bottom-up strategy combines many lesser things into a larger group of greater things. This coarse graining improves certainty because you end up with fewer things, or a reduction of detail. The space of possible outcomes is always shrinking.

We are often taught to think top-down, in a kind of divide-and-conquer strategy. This is the opposite of aggregation: it is a branching process. It starts with a root, or point of departure, and diverges exponentially into a great number of outcomes. How could one be sure of something in an exponentially diverging space of outcomes?

For promises to lead to certainty, they need to be noncontentious (see Chapter 6). Promises can coexist as long as they do not overlap or tread on each others' toes. Avoiding conflict between agents leads to certainty in a group. Ultimately Promise Theory makes conflict resolution easy.

Because agents are autonomous and can promise only their own behaviour, they cannot inflict outcomes on other agents (impositions try to do this, but can be ignored, at least in principle).

- If a single agent promises (offers or +) two things that are in conflict, it knows because it has all the information; it can resolve because it has all the control.

- If an agent accepts (uses or -) or uses two promises that are in conflict, it is aware because it has accepted them; it has all the information and all the control to stop accepting one.

In other words, the strategy of autonomy puts all of the information in one place. Autonomy makes infomation local. This is what brings certainty.

Some Exercises

1. Look at the examples of (+) and (-) promises, in "Cooperation: The Polarity of Give and Take" on page 26. For each (+) promise, what would be the matching (-) promise, and vice versa?

2. Now think of an IT project to build a server array for your latest software. The purpose of this thought experiment is to try making predictions along and against the grain of causation.

   How might you go about specifying requirements for the server array? For example, would you start from an expectation of usage demand? Would you base the requirements on a limited budget? Does this help you design an architecture for the server array? How can you decide what hardware to buy from this?

   Now instead of thinking about requirements, look at some hardware catalogues for servers and network gear. Look at the device specifications, which are promises. From these promises, can you determine what kind of hardware you need to buy? How can you predict what service level the hardware will deliver? Does this change your architectural design?

   Try going in the opposite direction and rewrite the hardware promises from the catalogue as project requirements. Does this make sense? Would it be possible to require twice the specifications than what you see in the catalogue? If so, how would you go about fulfilling those requirements?

3

Assessing Promises

The value of promising depends entirely on how it is assessed. Assessment of promises is an inherently subjective matter. Each agent may arrive at a different assessment, based on its observations. For instance, "I am/am not satisfied with the meal at the restaurant." Agent 1 might have the gene allele that makes cilantro/coriander taste like soap, while agent 2 is a devoted Thai food enthusiast extraordinaire. Assessments must therefore respect the individuality or *relativity* of different agents' perspectives.

What We Mean by Assessment

When we make a promise, we often have in mind a number of things:

- The promise itself: what outcome we intend

- The algorithm used to keep it: how a promise will be kept

- The motive behind it: why a promise is made

- The context in which it's kept: where, when a promise is made

Someone assessing a promise might care about exactly how a promise is kept, but the promiser may or may not promise to use a particular method. In that case, the precise method becomes a part of the intended outcome too, and there might be unfulfilled expectations of promises broken by failing to follow a very specific sequence of actions. Similarly, there are corresponding elements of assessing whether a promise has been kept.

- Outcome: What was measured during the assessment?
- Context: Where was the sample taken?
- Algorithm: How was the sample taken?
- Motive: Why the assessment was made?
- Expectation: What were we expecting to find?

Every promise is assessable in some way. Indeed, from the time a promise is made, a process of assessment begins in all agents that are in scope. This assessment may or may not be rational, but it is part of an ongoing estimation.

We humans often make assessments based on no evidence at all. Trust and even prejudice can form the basis for expectation. One might say: "When I release the hammer, it falls. This has always happened before, I see no reason why it would not happen now." In a familiar context, this assessment might be reliable; in outer space, it would be false. Whether inference is useful or not depends on a separate assessment of its relevance. Hearsay and authority are crutches we use to bootstrap trust.

Kinds of Promise Assessment

We often need to define what we mean by acceptable terms for a promise being kept. The reason might be grounded in legal process or simply be systemic rigour. Some kind of question needs to be answered.

An assessment of a promise may be based on any method, impression, or observation, that maps to the promise being "kept" or "not kept" at a certain time.

The reason this description is so loose is that humans are not very mechanistic in our evaluation of trust, and the assessment of a promise has a lot to do with how we perceive the agent supposedly keeping the promise.

We might have technical methods of assessing the promises made by a machine, such as compliance with road safety standards, or software testing probes. Then, assessment behaves like some kind of function to evaluate. On the other hand, we might have an entirely heuristic approach to deciding whether a party was good or bad.

The assessment itself makes a promise, namely one to supply its determination of the outcome; thus, it is not strictly a new kind of object in the theory of promises. The "impressions" could be points of data that are invented, received, or specifically measured about the promise. These might include evidence from measurements or even hearsay from other agents.

It is useful to define two particular assessments of outcome. These correspond roughly to the two interpretations of statistical data: namely a belief (Bayesian) interpretation, and a frequentist or evidential interpretation.

- A belief assessment made without direct observation

- An evidential assessment made with partial information

There are three outcomes of an assessment of whether or not a promise is kept:

- True

- False

- Indeterminate

Assessments are made by observing or sampling at a localized moment in time. In other words, an assessment is an event in time and space that samples an outcome that may or may not persist. Even when conditions have been assessed as making a promise kept or not kept, the promise made by the assessment itself has limited trustworthiness, as the system might have changed immediately after the assessment was made.[1]

Relativity: Many Worlds, Branches, and Their Observers

Agents' perspectives are what we refer to as agent relativity. Each agent has its own private world view. Agents privately assess whether they consider that promises have been kept in their own world. They also assess the *value* associated with a promise, in their view.

---

1 Even the physical sciences struggle with this kind of issue. In quantum mechanics, the state of a microscopic region of space can be known only at the moment it is sampled, and the likelihood of knowing its state thereafter depends on precise promises encoded into its mathematical description.

One of the things that makes a promise viewpoint advantageous is that we cannot easily brush these differences of assessment under the rug, as so often happens in other modelling frameworks. By forcing ourselves to confront agent individualities (and if necessary, make agents promise conformity), we find important lessons about the fragilities in our assumptions.

Confronting Viewpoints

Information systems today have to confront relative viewpoints in a number of ways. One of the most obvious examples concerns the freshness of data that spans the globe. This is called the *data consistency* problem. Data arrives at many different locations, and is distributed to other locations for viewing. It is cached or buffered to share the burden of access. An agent in the US and an agent in Europe might not see the same history of changes at all times because the information takes a finite time to travel. Much effort is expended in IT to try to promise consistent data for all. Sometimes, living without that promise is simpler. Then we speak of *eventual consistency*. Thinking in promises helps to unravel different viewpoints, whatever they might be.

This does not only apply to the obvious assessments: kept or not kept. A promise to give something is often seen as having a positive value to the recipient and a negative value or cost to the agent keeping the promise. An imposition, on the other hand, often carries a cost to the recipient, and brings value to the imposing agent.

This idea of promise valuation further implies that there can be competition between agents. If different suppliers in a market make different promises, then an assessment of their relative value can lead to a competition, or even a conflict of interest.

Relativity and Levels of Perception

Sometimes a relative perspective depends more on what level you interact with something than where and when. Imagine evaluating whether a book, a radio, or a hotel keeps its promises.

These agencies can be decomposed into parts on many levels. Should we assess whether each component keeps its promise (for example, in the radio, do components properly move around electrical currents), or should we rather ask whether the boxed arrangement of components keeps its promise to blast out music?

First, we have to decide at which level we intend to consume the promises, and who is the observer making the assessment?

Inferred Promises: Emergent Behaviour

The radio or music player is a nice example of a collective agency with emergent behaviour. It is an agency formed from multiple components that collectively promise something apparently new. The radio functionality does not come from any single component in the radio; it only appears when all of the components are working together as intended. However, not all systems that exhibit identifiable behaviours were designed explicitly with any promises in mind.

Some systems only appear to an observer to act as though they keep certain promises, when in fact no such promises have been made. The observer might either be out of the scope of the promise, but can still observe its repercussions, or in fact, no such promise might have been made at all.

- This car veers to the left.

- The traffic gets congested around rush hour.

- The computer tends to slow down if you run these programs together.

We call such effects *emergent*. In some cases, there might be promises of which we are not aware. Agents have information only about the existence of promises for which they are in scope. Someone might have promised one person without telling another. A design specification for a tool might not be in the public domain: "Take it or leave it."

Does this matter? From the perspective of an observer, naturally it makes no difference whether a promise has actually been made or not, as long as the agent appears to be behaving as though one has been made. It is entirely within the observer's rights to postulate a model for the behaviour in terms of hypothetical promises.

This is how science talks about the laws of nature. We can take scientific law to mean that the world appears to make certain behavioural promises, which we can codify into laws, because they are invariably kept. In truth, of course, no such laws have been passed by any legal entity. Nature seems to keep these promises, but no such promises are evident or published by nature in a form that allows us to say that they have been made. Nevertheless, we trust these promises to be kept.

So, based on its own world of incomplete information, any agent is free to postulate promised behaviour in other agents as a model of their behaviour. This hypothesis can also be assessed in the manner of a promise to self.

From any assessment, over an interval of time, an agent may infer the existence of one or more promises that seem to fit its assessment of the behaviour, regardless of whether such a promise has been made outside of its scope.

The observer cannot know whether its hypothesis is correct, even if an explanation is promised by the observed agent; it can only accumulate evidence to support the hypothesis.

For example, suppose a vending machine is observed to give out a chocolate bar if it receives a coin of a certain weight. Since most coins have standard weights and sizes, a thief who is not in possession of this knowledge might hypothesize that the machine actually promises to release a chocolate bar on receiving an object of a certain size. Without further evidence or information, the thief is not able to distinguish between a promise to accept a certain weight and a promise to accept a certain size, and so he might then attempt to feed objects of the right size into the machine to obtain the chocolate bar. Based on new evidence, he might alter his hypothesis to consider weight. In truth, both hypotheses might be wrong. The machine might in fact internally promise to analyze the metal composition of the coin, along with its size and other features.

Judging a Book by Its Cover

Sometimes we use the agency of packaging to make emergent behaviours explicit. For example, a radio is placed inside a box that has been designed to say "Radio!" Sometimes we lie about this, for example, when M gives James Bond a camera that looks like a pen. The container, or packaging, is a component that is added to specifically make the collective behaviour explicit. This is the promise of marketing.

How Promises Define Agent-Perceived Roles

The simplest kind of emergent behaviour is falling into a role. A *role* is just a pattern consisting of an unspecified agent or group of agents making certain promises. An agent that is aware of the promises, and assesses them, would be able to infer the pattern and name the role.

Roles are just names for patterns of promised behaviour, without necessarily being attached to a specific person or thing. For example, the role of doorstop can be promised by tables, chairs, hooks, or wedges of paper. In business, the role of developer or manager might be assumed by the same person in different contexts, based on what promises they keep. There are three ways that roles can be defined based on promises:

Role by appointment

> An agent is pointed to the same kind of promise by several other agents (Figure 3-1). For example, if 20 agents promise to send data to a single agent, that agent clearly has the role of "the agent to whom data is sent," which we might call a database, or a storage array, and so on. Similarly, we might identify the same agent by virtue of its promising to receive data from the 20 agents. In either case, the agent is a concentration of arrows of the same kind.

Figure 3-1. Role by appointment is when promises point in the same way to a particular kind of agent.

Role by association

> When an agent just happens to make a particular kind of promise, for example, web server or policeman. Suppose three different shops promise to sell smartphones. Then, by virtue of making the same promise, we see that this is a "thing" (i.e., a repeated pattern; see Figure 3-2). Thus, regardless of what they think themselves, every observer who can see the pattern can assign to the shops the role of smartphone vendors.

Figure 3-2. Role by association is when all agents make the same promise. In this case, it could be an emergent promise like a property of the agent (its gender).

Role by cooperation

When agents promise to work together as a unit (e.g., agents that promise to behave in concert, such as a number of soldiers working as a team; see Figure 3-3). The agents all promise to be alike, or behave in the same way, so that they become interchangeable. Alternatively, imagine that each team member has its own specialization, and promises to play its part to keep the collective promise of the whole team. This is the same as inanimate components in a radio making different promises, collectively promising the listener to form a collective design. Cooperative promises are the glue that allow a number of components to come together to form a collective *superagent*, with its own effective promise. The cooperative role is identified by promises that effectively say, "I belong to team X."

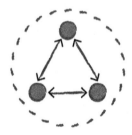

Figure 3-3. Role by cooperation is when agents play a part within a group.

Roles and Weak Coupling Prevent Paralysis

When agents or actors know their promised roles, but retain their basic autonomy, including unconstrained freedoms, they can get on with keeping those promises without waiting for outcomes that are the responsibilty of others. This is a very pragmatic way of avoiding paralysis and deadlock in systems. Strongly coupled systems have catastrophic failure modes and deadlocks because a small failure is transmitted rigidly to other agents.

One of the key insights of theories of autonomous parts, like promises, is that fine-grained autonomy allows a system to seek new solutions without being over-constrained. As an architectural principle, imagine architecting an adaptive ecology, rather than architecting a machine. A machine cannot search for a new pattern, but a dynamic ecology can.

The Economics of Promise Value: Beneficial Outcomes

Promises are valuable in a number of ways. They offer predictability, which is a valuable commodity because our expectations make it cheaper to operate. If we don't know what to expect, we have to be much more careful, and we might miss opportunities. Indeed, we would be experimenting all the time. Promises also offer delegation of responsibilty, at least partially. If another agent is willing to do something we rely on, that is valuable. Promises align our thinking in the direction of causation, instead of against it.

The reason we make promises at all is because they predict beneficial outcomes in the eye of some beholder. They offer information that might allow those who know about the promise to prepare themselves and win advantage. Physical law enables engineering, consistent bodily responses allow medicine, software promises data integrity, and so on.

Perhaps this makes you think of promising something to a friend, but don't forget to think about the more mundane promises we take for granted: a coffee shop serves coffee (not bleach or poison). The post office will deliver your packages. The floor beneath you will support you, even on the twenty-third level. If you could not rely on these things, life would be very hard.

A more difficult question is: what is this knowledge worth? Now, convention drives us to think that value means money, but that is not true at all. Money itself is simply a promise, represented by surrogate hardware like coins and paper, but value is a many-headed beast.[2] We offer one another value in many ways:

---

2 Pound notes, in the UK, still bear the text: "I promise to pay the bearer on demand the sum of X pounds." This goes back to the time when there was a trade-for-gold standard in money, and one could take the paper note to the Bank of England and be remunerated in gold. The gold standard no longer exists, but the principle remains.

- Money: a placeholder for value, to be redeemed later
- Credit: fictitious money
- Trade: equivalent value
- Goodwill: the opportunity to interact again
- In kind: returned favours, promises, gifts, etc.

The success of money lies in its promise to be a lingua franca for value exchange. It is an alchemist's dream: a form of value that everyone wants, and endlessly convertible.

As usual, the view of the autonomous agent is the key to understanding the relativity of value in Promise Theory. Every agent is free to decide the value of a promise, in whatever currency it deems valuable. We see this in the global economics of monetary currencies. The value of the dollar relative to, say, the yen is simply what others are willing to pay or exchange for dollars at any given moment. This is an assessment based on the promise of the currency's value in the eye of the beholder.

In Chapter 6, we'll see how repeated cooperation between agents builds trust and value, and plays an important role in motivating collaborative behaviour.

Human Reliability

Humans treat promises with the sort of casual abandon that sometimes shocks. We say "I promise" when, in fact, we have no intention to make any effort. This is compounded by the fact that humans are incalculable: our world views are all so different and individual that it is hard to reason about human behaviour as we try to do for simple-minded abstract "agents."

We are bombarded with information that makes us change our minds, on a timescale that makes us appear unreliable or fickle. Humans make promises into deceptions or lies on purpose, and often pursue self-interest in spite of making promises to cooperate as a team. This leads to a semantic chaos of fluctuating outcomes, not just a dynamical chaos of whether or not certain well-known promises are kept.

How can we even be sure what is being promised? Documentation of intent used to be considered a must, but then we discovered that promises could be made by appeal to intuition instead. Intuition taps into the cultural training we've all received, so we can rely on the promise of cultural norms to short-circuit expectation.

Culture and Its Promises

Culture brings with it a shared memory that we can assume everyone is aware of. This is often a shortcut when communicating. We use cultural context all the time when making promises. For example, when we see a green button next to a red button, we make a general assumption that the green button promises to start something and the red button promises to stop it. We draw on such references a lot when communicating. This is not part of Promise Theory, per se, but it relates to how explicitly we have to communicate intent, and whether everyone in a system of promises will make the same assessments. Market branding is an example of culturally primed promises by association.

If one could set aside the unreliable aspects of humanity to act as part of a reliable mechanism, there would be no impediment to success in designing human-technology systems, with dependable promises. But we are often unwilling to give up the freedoms we consider to be an essential part of humanity. During the industrial revolution, humans really did sacrifice their humanity to become part of the machine, and many were happy doing so in sweatshops. Today, we consider this to be dehumanizing.

How can we deal with these issues? Ultimately, we have to appeal to psychology to understand the likelihood of humans keeping promises in the manner of a chemistry of intent. This is true even for promises made by proxy through technology. The promise patterns for consistency reveal the ways to find consensus. Instead of single point agents, we might talk about a strong leader. Instead of a clique of a complete graph of agreements, we might talk about weak consensus.

The Eye of the Beholder

I once had a disagreement with someone about the nature of beauty. From a Promise Theory perspective, beauty is in the eye of the beholder. It is that simple. My opponent made an imposition argument against this, saying that we cannot ignore cultural norms when judging the value of something.

From a Promise Theory perspective, this is simple: each autonomous agent can indeed reject the weight of opinion and peer pressure because it is autonomous. Just as we are not obliged to accept the will of a mob, in principle. In practice, we might find it practical to do so, or we might feel weak and intimidated, fearing the consequences. However, this is an autonomous decision to comply. A stubborn person has the ability to resist.

Even if you believe that it is impossible to disregard peer pressure, mob rule, or other coercion,[3] there is still a plain engineering utility to adopting the autonomous agent model. Now you can model someone who is affected by mob rule as a person who always promises to follow the mob, while a free spirit is someone who doesn't. Thus the promise methodology allows you to model these differences and account for them. As in all science and engineering, we shouldn't muddle belief with utility.

Some Exercises

1. If someone leaves a package on your doorstep, do you consider the promise to deliver it kept?

2. There are many kinds of smartphones on the market that promise the Android operating system or Apple's iOS operating system. These are sufficient promises for many to think of the promised role of the smartphone, but not all of these devices can make calls. What promises distinguish the role of the smartphone from a tablet?

3. Branding is a form of culturally primed promise. The idea is to build familiarity with a simple image, such as the label on a bottle of wine. But how do we assess this promise over time? Lindeman's from Australia make a popular brand of wine. Does Lindeman's Bin 45 2012 promise the same as Lindemans's Bin 45 from 2010? Should we consider the brand a role by association?

4. Many websites promise secure payment facilities. How do you assess whether a payment system is secure? Do you look for a URL starting with

---

3 One way to define an attack is to impose an agent, without a promise to accept, and with the intent to cause harm.

https:, or perhaps a certificate signed by a known authority? What promises do these symbols represent? Are they sufficient?

5. In music, different voices promise different roles within a performance, such as melody, timekeeping rhythm, and ornamentation. Which instruments or voices play these roles in the following?

    a. Symphonic music (e.g., Richard Strauss, *Also sprach Zarathustra,* well known as the theme from *2001: A Space Odyssey*)

    b. Disco music

    c. Folk music

4

Conditional Promises —and Deceptions

Not all promises are made without attached conditions. For instance, we might promise to pay for something "cash on delivery" (i.e., only after a promised item has been received). Such promises will be of central importance in discussing processes, agreements, and trading.

The Laws of Conditional Promising

The truth or falsity of a condition may be promised as follows. An agent can promise that a certain fact is true (by its own assessment), but this is of little value if the recipient of the promise does not share this assessment.

- I promise X only if condition Y is satisfied.

A promise that is made subject to a condition that is not assessable cannot be considered a promise. However, if the state of the condition that predicates it has also been promised, completing a sufficient level of information to make an assessment, then it can be considered a promise. The trustworthiness of the promise is up to the assessing agent to decide. So there is at least as much trust required to assess conditionals as there is for unconditional promises.

We can try to state this as a rule:

A conditional promise cannot be assessed unless the assessor also sees that the condition itself is promised.

I call this *quenching* of the conditionals. Conversely:

If the condition is promised to be false, the remaining promise is rendered empty, or worthless.

A conditional promise is not a promise unless the condition itself is also promised.

Note that because promising the truth of a condition and promising some kind of service are two different types of promises, we must then deduce that both of these promises are (i) made to and from the same set of agents, and therefore (ii) calibrated to the same standards of trustworthiness. Thus, logically we must define it to be so.

We can generalize these thoughts for promises of a more general nature by using the following rules.

Local Quenching of Conditionals

If a promise is provided, subject to the provision of a prerequisite promise, then the provision of the prerequisite by the same agent is completely equivalent to the unconditional promise being made:

- I promise X if Y.
- I promise Y, too.

This combination is the same as "I promise X unconditionally." The regular rules of good old simplistic Boolean logic now apply within the same agent. If they didn't, we would consider the agent irrational.

This appeal to *local* logic gives us a rewriting rule for promises made by a single agent in the promise graph. The + is used to emphasize that X is being offered, and to contrast this with the next case.

Assisted Promises

Consider now a case in which one agent assists another in keeping a promise. According to our axioms, an agent can only promise its own behaviour, thus the promise being made comes only from the principal agent, not the assistant. The assistant might not even be known to the final promisee.[1] Assistance is a matter of voluntary cooperation on the part of the tertiary agent.

So, if a promise is once again provided, subject to the promise of a prerequisite condition, then the quenching of that condition by a separate *assistant* agent might also be acceptable, provided the principal promiser also promises to acquire the service from the assistant.

- I promise X if Y.

- I have been promised Y.

- I promise to use Y is now equivalent to "I can probably promise X."

Notice that, when quenched by an assistant, the trustworthiness is now an assessment about multiple agents, not merely the principal. A recipient of such a promise might assess the trustworthiness of the promise differently, given that other agents are involved, so it would be questionable (even a lie or deception) to reduce the three promises to a single promise of X, without qualification. The promises are similar, but not identical, as the assessment takes into account the uncertainties in the information provided.

I call this an assisted promise.

Conditional Causation and Dependencies

If we are trying to engineer a series of beneficial outcomes, telling a story in a simple linear fashion, preconditions are a useful tool. Sometimes people refer to this kind of arrangement of promises as choreography or even orchestration.

There are many examples of technology that make promises conditional on dependencies (Figure 4-1). Electrical devices that use batteries are an example. Software is often packaged in such a way as to rely on the presence of other components. Some packages do not even make it clear that their promises are conditional promises: they deceive users by not telling whether promises are conditional, so that one cannot judge how fragile they are before trying to install them.

---

1 When a conditional promise is made and quenched by an assistant, the "contact" agent is directly responsible by default. We shall refine this view with alternative semantics later, since this is all a matter of managing the uncertainty of the promise being kept. As soon as we allow rewriting rules of this basic type, it is possible to support multiple solutions for bringing certainty with graded levels of complexity.

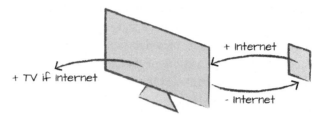

Figure 4-1. A conditional promise, conditional on a dependency, such as a television whose service depends on the promise of an Internet connection from the wall socket.

Circular Conditional Bindings: The Deadlock Carousel

Deadlocks occur when agents make conditions on each other so that no actual promise is given without one of the two relaxing its constraints on the other. For instance:

- Agent 1 promises X if Agent 2 keeps promise Y.

- Agent 2 promises Y if Agent 1 keeps promise X.

The dragon swallows its tail! This pair of promises represents a standoff or deadlock. One of the two agents has to go first. Someone has to break the symmetry to get things moving.

It is like two mistrusting parties confronting one another: hand over the goods, and I'll give you the money! No, no, if you hand over the money, I'll give you the goods (Figure 4-2).

Figure 4-2. A deadlock: I'll go, if you go first!

Interestingly, if you are a mathematician, you might recognize that this deadlock is exactly like an equation. Does the righthand side determine the lefthand side, or does the lefthand side determine the righthand side? When we solve equations, we end up not with a solution but with a generator of solutions. It is only when we feed in a boundary condition that it starts to generate a stream of solutions like a never-ending motor.

The same is true of these promises. If one of the agents can't just go first, and remove its blocking condition, then the cycle continues to go around and never generates the end result (see Figure 4-3). If the promise is a one-off (a so-called idempotent operation) then it quickly reaches its final state. If the promise is repeatable, then Agent 1 will continue to give X to agent 2, and agent 2 (on receiving X) will respond with Y to agent 1. Curiously, the deadlock is actually the generator of the desired behaviour, like a motor, poised to act.

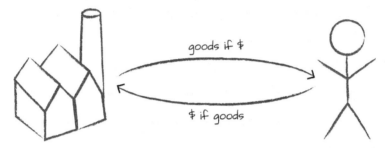

Figure 4-3. Circular dependencies — trust issues: you get the goods when we see the money, or you'll get the money when we see the merchandise!

The Curse of Conditions, Safety Valves

The matter of deadlocks shows us that conditions are a severe blocker to cooperative behaviour. Conditions are usually introduced into promises because an agent does not trust another agent to keep a promise it relies on. The first agent wants to hedge its own promise so it does not appear to be responsible or liable for the inability for it to keep its own promise. Recall that a conditional promise is not really a promise at all, unless the condition has also been promised.

In the next chapter, we'll see how work from cooperative game theory shows that agents can win over the long term when they remove conditions and volunteer their services without demanding up-front payment. Conditional strategies like "tit for tat" are successful once cooperation is ongoing, but if one agent fails to deliver for some reason, tolerance of the faults keeps the cooperation going, rather than have it break down into a standoff again. Examples of this can been seen in everything from mechanical systems to international politics. The utility of Promise Theory here is in being able to see what is common across such a wide span of agency.

So what is the point of conditions? If they only hinder cooperation, why do we bother at all? One answer is that they act as a long-term safety valve (i.e., a kind of dead-man's brake) if one agent in a loop stops keeping its promise. A condition would stop other agents from keeping their promise without reciprocation, creating an asymmetry that might be perceived as unfair, or even untenable. Thus, conditions become useful once a stable trade of promises is ongoing. First, a relationship needs to get started.

Other Circular Promises

The case above is the simplest kind of loop in a promise, but we can make any loops with any number of agents. How can we tell if these promises can lead to a desired end state? For example:

- 1 promises to drive 2 if 3 fixes 1's car.

- 2 promises to lend 3 a tool if 1 drives 2.

- 3 promises to fix 1's car if 2 will lend a tool.

Such examples may or may not have a solution. In this case, there is another deadlock that can only be resolved by having one of the agents keep its promise without any condition. The conditions could be added back later.

Some circular promises can be consistent in the long run, but need to be started by breaking the deadlock with some initial voluntary offsetting of a condition. The three promises above are a case in point. Assuming all three agents are keeping these promises on a continuous basis, it all works out, but if someone is waiting out of mistrust for evidence of the other, it will never get started. Readers who are programmers, steeped in imperative thinking, should beware of thinking of promises with conditionals as being just like flowcharts.

A simple answer to this is average consistency from graph theory. So-called eigenvalue solutions, or fixed points of the maps, are the way to solve these problems for self-consistency. Game theory's Nash equilibrium is one such case. Not all problems of this kind have solutions, but many do. A set of promises that does not have a solution will not lead to promises kept, so it will be a failure. I don't want to look at this matter in any more depth. Suffice it to say that there is a well-known method for answering this question using the method of *adjacency matrices* for the network of promise bindings. The fixed-point methodology allows us to frame bundles of promises as self-sustaining mathematical games. There are well-known tools for solving games.

Logic and Reasoning: The Limitations of Branching and Linear Thinking

Conditions like the ones above form the basis of Boolean reasoning. It is the way we learn to categorize outcomes and describe pathways. This form of reasoning grew up in the days of ballistic warfare, where branching outcomes from ricochets and cannonballs hitting their targets were the main concerns.

This "if-then-else" framework is the usual kind of reasoning we learn in school. It is a serial procedure, based on usually binary true/false questions. It leads to simple flowcharts and the kind of linear storyline that many find appealing.

Promises Are Declarative, Not Imperative

If you are reading this book, there is a good chance that you have learned computer programming, and are steeped in sequential flowchart thinking. If you are lucky, you've learned some parallel coding. The promises we are describing in this book are not mere programming steps, and you should resist the temptation to imagine you are reading about a programming methodology, or even a language construct.[2] Programming steps involve very narrow interpretations, but promises in general can be as broad as we like.

Boolean logic is not the only kind of reasoning, however. Electronic circuits do not have to work with only two possible values; they can support a continuum of values, such as the volume control on your music player. In biology, DNA works with an alphabet of four states, and chemical signals work on cells by changing concentration gradients. In computer simulations, cellular automata

---

2 Some computer languages do have constructs called promises, but, although related, these are not precisely the same as the subject of this book.

perform computations and solve problems by emergent outcomes with no linear reasoning at all. Random, so-called Monte Carlo methods can answer questions by trial and error, like pinning a tail on the donkey.

Most of us are less well trained in the methods mentioned above, and thus we tend to neglect them when solving problems involving parallelism. I believe that is a mistake because the world at large is a parallel system.

The compelling thing about our ballistic reasoning is that it results in stories, like the kind that humans told around the fire for generations. Our attachment to stories is remarkable. The way we communicate is in linear narratives, so we tend to think in this way, too. If you have ever tried parallel programming or managing a team, you'll know that even though you serialize the outcomes in your planning and reporting, the work does not have to be done as an exact facsimile of the story you tell. We muddle the parallel in serial story lines.[3]

Serialization seems simpler than parallelization because we reason in that way as human beings. But the branching that is usually required in serial reasoning actually ends up increasing the final complexity by magnifying the number of possible outcomes (see Figure 4-4).

Whenever logical reasoning enters a problem, the complexity rises dramatically. Our present-day model of reasoning has its roots in ballistics, and often views unfolding processes as branches that diverge. You can see why in Figure 4-4.

Figure 4-4. Decisions lead to many possible worlds or outcomes, like a game of billiards. This is "ballistic reasoning" or deterministic reasoning.

The idea of a process with diverging possibilities is somewhat like the opposite of a promise converging on a definite outcome. So logic is a sort of sleeping enemy that we often feel we cannot do without.

---

3 This post hoc narrative issue is at the heart of many discussions about fault diagnosis. When things go wrong, it leads to a distorted sense of causation.

Convergence and Divergence

The if-then-else challenge leads to branching pathways in a system: each if-then-else decision contributes to new possible outcomes. Decisions thus reduce the likelihood that any one end state will be the outcome. The aim of promises is the opposite: to collapse all outcomes to a single defined state of things. Convergence, or coming together, also has an implicit *if*, but no *else*. It says that if we have arrived at the desired outcome, then do nothing. This is sometimes called *idempotence* in computing.[4]

Complexity begins with conditionals (i.e., the answer to a question that decides the way forward). In a sequence of promises, we might want something to be conditional on a promise being made or on a promise being kept. This means we need to think about verification and trust as basic parts of the story.

You might think that conditional promises look just like if-then-else computer programming, but no. An imperative computer program is a sequence of impositions, not promises. Most programming languages do not normally promise that something will be kept persistently; they deal in only transient states, throwing out requests, and leave the verification to the programmer. A sequence of conditional promises is more like a logistics delivery chain, which we'll discuss in the next chapter. Conditionals are the basis for cooperation.

Some Exercises

1. If you know a promise is contingent on some other agent's cooperation, how would you explain this to a promisee? If you make a promise without a condition, would this count as a deception?

2. Software packages are often installed with dependencies: you must install X before you can install Y. Express this as promises instead. What is the agent that makes the promise? Who is the promisee?

3. The data transfer rate indicated on a network connection is a promise made usually about the maximum possible rate. By not declaring what

---

4 This is inaccurate usage of the term idempotence, but it has already become a cultural norm.

that depends on, it can be deceptive. Suggest a more realistic promise for a network data rate, taking into account the possible obstacles to keeping the promise, like errors, the counterpart's capabilities, and so on.

5

Engineering Cooperation

Promising to work with peers is what we call cooperation. Promise Theory exposes cooperation as an exercise in information sharing. If we assess those other agents' promises to be trustworthy, we can rely on them and use that as a basis for our own behaviour. This is true for humans, and it is true for technological proxies.

The subject of cooperation is about coordinating the behaviours of different autonomous agents, using promises to signal intent. We see the world as more than a collection of parts, and dare to design and construct larger, intentional systems that behave in beneficial ways.

Engineering Autonomous Agents

There are many studies of cooperation in the scientific literature from differing viewpoints. To make a claim of engineering, we propose to think in terms of tools and a somewhat precise language of technical meanings. This helps to minimize the uncertainty when interpreting agents' promises and behaviours. Cooperation involves a few themes:

- Promises and intentions (the causes)
- Agreement
- Cooperation
- Equilibration
- Behaviour and state (outcomes)

- Emergence

In this chapter, I want to paint a picture of cooperation as a process just like any other described in natural science by atomizing agency into abstract agents, and then binding them back together into a documentable way through the promises they advertise. In this way, we develop a chemistry of intent.

Promisees, Stakeholders, and Trading Promises

So far, we've not said much about the *promisees* (i.e., those agents to whom promises are made). In a sense, the promisee is a relatively unimportant part of promises, for many aspects, because the agent principally affected by a promise is the autonomous *promiser* itself. A promise is a self-imposition, after all.

The exception to this is when we consider cooperation between agents because of the *value* of recognizing whether their promises will be kept. When an agent assesses a promise as valuable (to itself), it becomes a stakeholder in its outcome. This is why we aim promises at particular individuals in the first place. Promises form a currency of cooperation. Anyone can observe a promise, and decide whether or not it was kept, without being directly affected by it, but only agents with a stake in the collaboration hold the outcome to be of particular importance.

Promisees and stakeholders have their moment when promises become part of a web of incentive and trade in the exchange of favours. Thus the subject of cooperation is perhaps the first place where the arrow in a promise finds its role.

Broken Promises

Cooperation is about the keeping of promises to stakeholders, but so far we've not mentioned what it means for promises to be broken. Most of us probably feel an intuitive understanding of this already, as we experience promises being broken every day. Nevertheless, it is useful to express this more clearly.

Our most common understanding of breaking a promise is that it can be *passively* broken. In other words, there is a promise that is not kept due to inaction, or due to a failure to keep the terms of the promise. To know when such a promise has not been kept, there has to be a time limit of some kind built into the promise. Once the time limit has been exceeded, we can say that the promise has not been kept. The time limit might be entirely in the perception of the agent assessing the promise, of course. Every agent makes this determination autonomously.

There is also an *active* way of breaking a promise. This is when an agent makes another promise that is in conflict with the first. If the second promise is incompatible with the first, in the view of the promisees or stakeholders, or the second promise prevents the promiser from keeping the first promise in any way, then we can also say that promises have been broken.

Broken promises thus span conflicts of interest, as well as failures to behave properly.

What Are the Prerequisites for Cooperation?

For autonomous agents to coordinate their intent, they need to be able to communicate proposals to one another. The minimum promise that an agent has to keep is therefore to accept proposals from other agents (i.e., to *listen*). From this starting point, any agent could impose proposals on another agent.

In a more civil arrangement, agents might replace impositions with promises to respond and alter proposals, forming an ongoing relationship between the agents. These ongoing relationships are the stable fodder of cooperation. They leave open a channel for negotiation and collaboration.

IT Networks as an Example of Cooperation

Networks exist for cooperation between agencies.

The agencies of IT networks are software, computers, interfaces, cables, switches, and routers. Software is a proxy for human intent, and it makes impositions and keeps promises on our behalf. The way these agencies connect together allows them to make certain promises to one another on our behalf. In other words, the promises made by the software are conditional on the promises of the communication infrastructure.

When using networks as examples of promise thinking, we have to be careful not to confuse cable connections with promise arrows.

Who Is Responsible for Keeping Promises?

From the first promise principle, agents are always responsible for keeping their own promises. No agent may make a promise on behalf of another. Regrettably, we are predisposed to think in terms of impositions and obligations, not promises, which pretend the exact opposite.

Impositions might not encourage cooperation at all (indeed they sometimes provoke stubborn opposition), but there is another way to win the influence of agents. As agents begin to trade promises with one another, there are indirect ways to encourage others to behave to our advantage, voluntarily, by promising their own behaviour in trade.

Agencies guide the outcomes of processes with different levels of involvement, and indeed different levels of success. This happens through incentives that work on behalf of self-interest. Agents might be "hands-on" (explicit) or "hands-off" (implicit) in their use of incentives, but in all cases their own promises exist to coax cooperative promises from others for individual benefit.

Every agent is thus responsible for carrying the burden of its own promises. In order to use Promise Theory as a tool for understanding cooperation, an engineer therefore needs to adjust his or her thinking to adopt the perspective of each individual agent in a system, one by one. This might be remarkably difficult to do, given our natural tendency to command the parts into compliance, but it pays off. The difference is that, when we look at the world from the perspective of the agencies, we begin to understand their limitations and take them into account. Practicing this way of thinking will cleanse the windows of perception on cooperative engineering, and change the way you think about orchestrating behaviour.

Distributed Cooperation by Network

The Internet is built on promises kept by many different agencies. Consider the Domain Name Service (DNS) as an example.

DNS is a service that promises to translate the names of places and services on the Internet into their addresses so that data can be delivered to them. It helps users find and use the services promised by other agencies. It is one of several *directory services* for the network: a service describing services.

The promise—to perform address lookup—is made voluntarily by those agencies that implement DNS. Specialized software agents keep the promise, dependent on the communication infrastructure, which involves many other promises working together.

DNS providers promise "authoritative information" about themselves for others to use. While no agent could be prevented from using their own alternative source of information, or even making up false information, there is usually little value in doing so, as the point is to look inside a site for personal use.

However, agents can also promise to redistribute address information—without misrepresenting it—to help accelerate lookups by end users. Occasionally, attackers abuse this trust to redirect users to false addresses. In this case, users have to rely on the promise of trusted site signatures to verify the authenticity of the place where they arrive.

Participants in DNS promise the availability of a *collective service*, of mutual value, entirely by *voluntary* and *mutual cooperation*. A similar story could be told about many other distributed services.

Mutual Bindings and Equilibrium of Agreement

Collaboration towards a shared outcome, or a common purpose, happens when we exchange information. This information especially includes promises to one another. The beginning of cooperation lies in agreeing about promise bindings (i.e., pairs of promises that induce agents to cooperate voluntarily).

As agents negotiate, there is a tug-of-war between opposing interests, from the promises they are willing to make themselves, to those they are willing to accept from their counterparts. The theory of games refers to this tug-of-war stalemate as a Nash equilibrium. This is technical parlance for a compromise.

The process by which everyone ends up agreeing on the same thing is thus called equilibration. In information technology, this is sometimes called a consensus. Equilibrium means balance (think of the zodiac sign Libra, meaning balance), and this balance brings an intrinsic stability to processes and outcomes (see Figure 5-1). Although, culturally, we invariably favour the notion of "winning," we should be very worried about making cooperative situations too one-sided.

The idea of winning and losing draws attention away from mutual cooperation and towards greed and instability. To have cooperation, we need a system of agents to form stable relationships. In other words, they need to keep their promises consistently, without wavering or changing their minds. The secret to balance is to find a formulation of mutual promises that each agent can maintain in a stable trade relationship with the others.

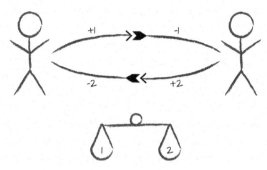

Figure 5-1. To talk bidirectionally and reach an equilibrium requires four promises! Promise bindings 1 and 2 must be assessed, by each agent, to be of acceptable return value in relation to the promise they give.

Cooperation as a Game

The theory of games, which Promise Theory draws on, points clearly to the idea that long-term success in trading promises can be accelerated by a short-term willingness to compromise on one's own selfish needs (i.e., to accept the other agent's perceived shortcomings without withholding one's own favours in return). This was the lesson we learned as the curse of the conditional promises. Conversely, if agents focus on short-term wins, at the expense of others, this can lead to a long-term collapse.

When one agent makes a promise to offer its service (+) and another accepts (-) that promise, it allows the first agent to pass information to the second. Both promises must be repeated in reverse other for the second agent to pass information back to the first.

This makes a total of four promises: two (+) and two (-). These promises form the basis for a common world view. Without that platform, it is difficult for agencies to work with common purpose.

Incompatible Promises: Conflicts of Intent

Some promises cannot be made at the same time. For instance, a door cannot promise to be both open and closed. A person cannot promise to be both in Amsterdam and New York at the same time. This can result in conflicts of intent.

Conflicts of giving (+)
> An agent can promise X or Y, but not both, while two other agents can promise to accept without conflict; for example, an agent promises to lend a book to both X and Y at the same time.

Conflicts of usage (-)
> A single agent promises to use incompatible promises X and Y from two different givers; for example, the agent promises to accept simultaneous flights to New York and Paris. The flights can both be offered, but cannot be simultaneously accepted.

Cooperating for Availability and the Redundancy Conundrum

One of the goals of systems and services, whether human-, mechanical-, or information-based, is to be reliable and predictable. Without a basic predictability, it is hard to make a functioning world. Although we haven't fully specified what the capabilities of a promise agent are, realistically there must be limits to what it can promise: no agency is all-powerful.

It's normal to call a single agent keeping a promise a *single point of failure*, because if, for whatever reason, it is either unable or unwilling to keep its promise, the promisee, relying on it, will experience a breach of trust. A design goal in the making of robust systems is to avoid single points of failure.

As usual, Promise Theory predicts two ways to improve the chances that a promise will be kept. The promiser can try harder to keep its (+) promise, and the promisee can try harder to secure its (-) promise to complete the binding. The issue is slightly different if, instead of a pre-agreed promise binding, the client imposes requests onto a promising agent without warning, as this indicates a divestment of responsibilty, rather than a partnership to cooperate.

One mechanism for improving availability is *repetition*, or *learning*, as agents in a promise binding keep their promises repeatedly. This is the value of rehearsal, or "practice makes perfect." The phrase *anti-fragile* has been used to describe systems that can strengthen their promise-keeping by trial and error. Even with rehearsals, there are limits to what a single agent can promise.

The principal strategy for improving availability is to increase the *redundancy* of the agencies that keep promises. If an agent is trying to work harder, it can club together with other agents and form agents aligned in a collaborative role to keep the promise. If a client is trying harder to obtain a promise, it can seek out more agents offering the same promise, whether they are coordinated or not.

Availability Is a Valued Promise

Branches of a shopping franchise collaborate on promising a consistent experience to shoppers (the promisees), but they don't always act as backups for one another in case one shop cannot be available. In the age of the Internet, however, online shopping should never be unavailable. Indeed, availability is almost considered an obligation.

Redundancy is the strategy for availability, as in Figure 5-2. In the simplest case, one ensures that every component has a backup. In IT, we speak of "failing over" to a redundant agent if our first choice is not available. As long as both agents make the same promises,[1] there should be no problem. However, we do have to know the location of the backup.

How do the agents know what the other promises? They make promises to one another to exchange that information. This adds vital promises that they need to keep (see Figure 5-2).

Let's consider the cases for redundancy in turn, with the specific example of trying to obtain a taxi from one or more taxi providers.

A single taxi agent (promiser) cannot promise to be available to offer a ride to every client at all times, but several taxis can agree to form a collaborative group, placing themselves in the role of the taxi company (a role by cooperation). The taxi company, acting as a single super-agency, now promises to be available at all times. This must be a gamble, based on how many agents make the promise to drive a taxi and how many clients promise to use the taxi by booking up front.

---

1 One agent should not promise something the other wouldn't; for example, it should not promise a "back-door" to a service.

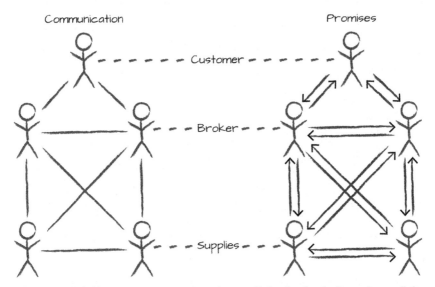

Figure 5-2. A stakeholder, wanting to use a promise provided redundantly, has to know all the possible agencies and their backups making the promise. It also wants a promise that all agents are equivalent, which means that those agencies need to promise to collaborate on consistency. These agents in turn might rely on other back-office services, provided redundantly, and so on, all the way down. Vertical promises are delegation promises, and horizontal promises are collaboration/coordination promises.

Clients can call any one of the taxis (as long as they know how to reach one of them), and enter into a promise binding that is conditional on finding a free car. The taxis can share the load between one another voluntarily, with a little pre-promised cooperative communication. If clients don't book ahead, but call without warning, planning is harder, as the imposition must be directed to a single agent for all the collaborators. This might be a call centre. If that single agent is unavailable, it pushes the responsibility back onto the imposer to try another agent. This, in turn, means that the imposer personally has to know about all the agents it could possibly impose upon. That might include different taxi companies (i.e., different collaborative groups of agents making a similar promise). See Figure 5-3.

When multiple agents collaborate on keeping the same promises, they have to promise to coordinate with one another. The collaboration promises are auxiliary to the promises they will make to stakeholders: individual inward-facing promises to support a collective outward-facing promise. Sharing the load of *impositions*, however, requires a new kind of availability, with a new single point of failure: namely, the availability of the "point of presence" or call centre. The call centre solves one problem of locating redundant promisers at the expense of an exactly similar problem for the intermediate agency. I call this the load-balancing conundrum.

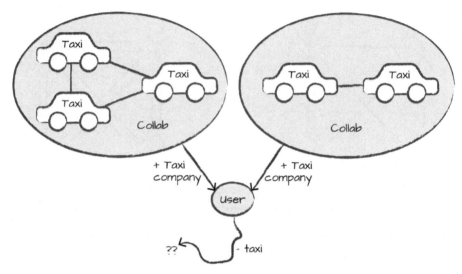

Figure 5-3. Different groups of taxis can collaborate in different groups to handle load by coopera-tion. Which provider should the user/stakeholder pick to keep the promise?

Now let's flip the point of view over to the taxi-promise user (-), or promisee, and recall the basic principle of promises, namely that the user always has the last word on all decisions, because no agent can impose decisions.

Promisees or stakeholders, needing a ride, experience a problem with *consuming* redundancy. Each time a promisee has more than one alternative, it has to decide which agent to go to for a promise binding, and thus needs to know how to find all of the agents making the promise. This choice is independent of whatever the providers promise. The selection does not have to be within the same collaborative group: it could be from a competing taxi company, or from an independent operator.[2]

---

2 In a case like this, agents don't usually broadcast their promises individually to potential users because that would be considered spam (in Internet parlance). Flood advertising is often unwelcome in our noisy society.

Again, one way to solve the problem of finding a suitable promiser, like the call centre, is to appoint an agent in the role of a *directory service*, broker, dispatcher, or load balancer (recall the DNS example, essentially like the phone book). This introduces a proxy agent, working on behalf of the user (we'll return to discuss proxies in more detail in the next chapter). However, this addition once again introduces a new single point of failure, which also needs to be made redundant to keep the promise of availability. That simply brings back the same problem, one level higher. One can imagine adding layer upon layer, getting nowhere at all. There is no escape. It's turtles all the way down.

What should be clear from the promise viewpoint is that the responsibility to find a provider always lies with the consumer. The consumer is the only acceptable single point of failure, because if it goes away, the problem is solved! The same arguments apply to load sharing in regards to availability. The conclusion is simple: introducing brokers and go-betweens might be a valid way to delegate, but in terms of redundancy, it makes no sense.

In software systems, it is common to divest responsibility and use middlemen load balancers, which introduce complexity and cost. The Promise Theory answer is simple: we should design software to know who to call. Software is best positioned to do its own load balancing, rather than relying on a proxy, but this means it needs to know all the addresses of all agents that can keep certain promises. Then, failing over, going to backup, or whatever we want to call it, has a maximum probability of delivering on the promise. Designing systems around promises rather than impositions leads to greater certainty.

Redundancy Cannot Be Given, Only Used

The conclusion that a consumer cannot buy availability should now be obvious from promise principles. Agents can only make promises about themselves. No agent can promise 100 percent availability (that would simply be a lie). So it is up to the consumer to arrange for 100% consumer access by having multiple providers. The redundancy is thus a result of usage, dependent on the promises being kept.

Agents working together can promise to work together to back one another up, but they cannot promise 100% even collectively, as something might come between them and the consumer that is beyond their control.

Agreement as Promises: Consensus of Intent

Agreement is a key element of cooperation. To collaborate on a common goal, we have to be able to agree on what that is. This usually involves exchanging proposals and decisions.

If agents promise to accept a proposal from another, then they attest to their belief in it. Suppose we have one or more agents promising to accept a promise. An observer, seeing such a promise to accept a proposal, could conclude that all of the agents (promising to accept the same proposal) in fact agreed about their position on this matter. So if there were three agents and only two agreed, it would look like Figure 5-4.

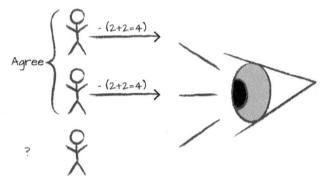

Figure 5-4. An observer sees two agents promise to use the same proposal, and hence agree. Nothing can be said about the third agent.

Agents, within some ensembles, may or may not know about their common state of agreement. However, an observer, privy to all the promises, observes a common pattern or role amongst the agents. The single agent making the promise accepted by the others assumes the role of a point of calibration for their behaviour.

When a promise proposal originates from another agent, accepting this proposal is an act of voluntary subordination (see Figure 5-5). If both agents trade such promises, the mutual subordination keeps a balance, like the tug-of-war we mentioned earlier.

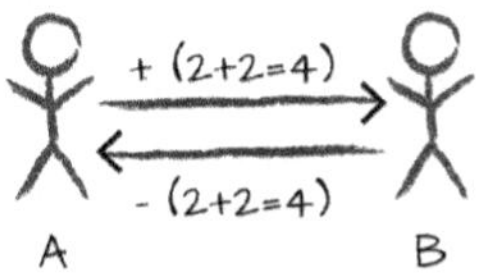

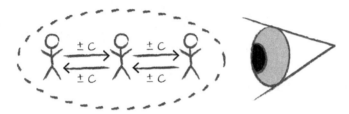

Figure 5-5. Agent B agrees with agent A's promised belief, subordinating to A. Here, only agent A can tell, because no one else sees B's promise to accept the assertion.

It might be surprising to notice that agreement is a one-way promise. It is, in fact, a role by association. Agreement is also an autonomous decision: a single promise to accept a proposal. If we want to go further and have consensus, we need to arrange for mutual agreement. Such equilibrium of intent is the key to cooperation. Indeed, if both agents agreed with one another, we might speak not only of mutual agreement, but of an intent to cooperate (see Figure 5-6).

Figure 5-6. Cooperation means that agents promise to agree with one another about some subject.

Contractual Agreement

The preceding interpretation of agreement solves one of the long-running controversies in philosophy about whether contracts are bilateral sets of promises. This is now simply resolved with the notion of a promise proposal. A proposal is the text or body of a promise, without it having been adopted or made by any agent. Promise proposals are an important stage in the lifecycle of promises that allows promises to be negotiated.

A contract is a bundle of usually bilateral *promise proposals* between a number of agents that is intended to serve as the body of an agreement. A contract is not a proper agreement until it has been accepted by all parties (i.e., until the parties agree to it). This usually happens by signing.

All legal agreements, terms, and conditions may be considered sets of promises that define hypothetical boundary conditions for an interaction between parties or agents. The law is one such example. One expects that the promises described in the terms and conditions of the contract will rarely need to be enforced, because one hopes that things will never reach such a point; however, the terms define a standard response to such infractions (threats). Legal contracts define what happens mainly at the edge states of the behaviour one hopes to ensue.

Service-level agreements, for example, are legal documents describing a relationship between a provider and a consumer. The body of the agreement consists of the promised behaviours surrounding the delivery and consumption of a service. From this, we may define a *service-level agreement* as an agreement between two agents whose body describes a contract for service delivery and consumption.

Contracts and Signing

The act of signing a proposal is very similar to agreement. It is a realization of an act (+) that has the effect of making a promise to accept (-). This is an example of reinterpretation by a dual promise of the opposite polarity.

A signature thus behaves as a promise by the signing agent to use or accept a proposed bundle of promises. It is realized typically by attaching an agent's unique identity, such as a personal mark, DNA, or digital key. During a negotiation, many promise proposals might be put forward, but only the ones that are signed turn into real promises (see Figure 5-7).

Figure 5-7. A signature is a promise to accept a proposal.

For example, when a client signs an insurance contract, he or she agrees about the proposed content, and the contract comes into force by signing. What about the countersigning by the insurance company? Sometimes this is explicit, sometimes implicit. If there is no explicit countersigning, one presumes that the act of writing the contract proposal on company letterhead counts as a sufficient signature or implicit promise to accept the agreement. However, one could imagine a dispute in which the insurer tried to renege on the content of a contract (e.g., by claiming it was written by a rogue employee on their company paper).

Explicit promises help clarify both the process and limitations of an agreement. Each party might promise asymmetrically to keep certain behaviours, but the overlap is the only part on which they agree.

Agreement in Groups

One of the problems we face in everyday life, both between humans and between information systems, is how to reach an agreement when not all agents are fully in the frame of information. For instance, the following is a classic problem from distributed computing that we can all identify with. The classic solutions to these problems in computing involve *protocols* or agreed sequences of commands.[3] A command-oriented view makes this all very complicated and uncertain, so let's take a promise-oriented viewpoint.

Suppose four agents—A, B, C, and D—need to try to come to a decision about when to meet for dinner. If we think in terms of command sequences, the following might happen:

1. A suggests Wednesday to B, C, and D.
2. In private, D and B agree on Tuesday.
3. D and C then agree that Thursday is better, also in private.
4. A talks to B and C, but cannot reach D to determine which conclusion was reached.

This might seem like a trivial thing. We just check the time, and the last decision wins. Well, there are all kinds of problems with that view. First of all, without D to confirm the order in which the conversations with B and C occurred, A only has the word of B and C that their clocks were synchronized and that they were telling the truth (see Figure 5-8).

---

3 Technologies such as vector clocks and Paxos, for instance.

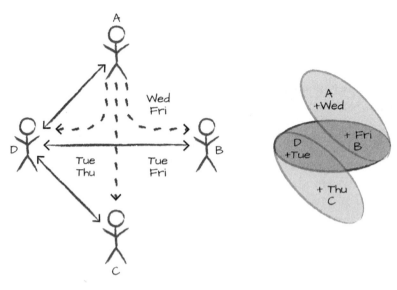

Figure 5-8. Looking for a Nash equilibrium for group agreement.

A is unable to find out what the others have decided, unable to agree with them by signing off on the proposal. To solve this, more information is needed by the agents. The Promise Theory principles of autonomous agents very quickly show where the problem lies. To see why, let's flip the perspective from agents telling one another when to meet, to agents telling one another when they can promise to meet. Now they are talking about only themselves, and what they know.

1. A promises he can meet on Wednesday to B, C, D.
2. D and B promise each other than they can both meet on Tuesday.
3. D and C promise each other that they can both meet on Thursday.
4. A is made aware of the promises by B and C, but cannot reach D.

Each agent knows only what promises he has been exposed to. So A knows he has said Wednesday, and B, C, and D know this too. A also knows that B has said Tuesday and that C has said Thursday, but doesn't know what D has promised.

There is no problem with any of this. Each agent could autonomously meet at the promised time, and they would keep their promises. The problem is only that the intention was that they should all meet at the same time. That intention was a group intention, which has not been satisfied. Somehow, this must be communicated to each agent individually, which is just as hard as the problem of deciding when to meet for dinner. Each agent has to promise (+) his intent, and accept (-) the intent of the others to coordinate.

Let's assume that the promise to meet one another (above) implies that A, B, C, and D all should meet at the same time, and that each agent understands this. If we look again at the promises above, we see that no one realizes that there is a problem except for D. To agree with B and C, he had to promise to accept the promise by B to meet on Tuesday, and accept to meet C on Thursday. These two promises are incompatible. So D knows there is a problem, and is responsible for accepting these promises (his own actions). So theoretically, D should not accept both of these options, and either B or C would not end up knowing D's promise.

To know whether there is a solution, a God's-eye view observation of the agents (as we, the readers, have) only needs to ask: do the intentions of the four agents overlap at any time (see the righthand side of Figure 5-8)? We can see that they don't, but the autonomous agents are not privy to that information. The solution to the problem thus needs the agents to be less restrictive in their behaviour and to interact back and forth to exchange the information about suitable overlapping time. This process amounts to the way one would go about solving a game-theoretic decision by Nash equilibrium.

With only partial information, progress can still be made if the agents trust one another to inform each other about the history of previous communications.

1. A promises he can meet on Wednesday or Friday to B, C, and D.

2. D and B promise each other than they can both meet on Tuesday or Friday, given knowledge of item 1.

3. D and C promise each other that they can both meet on Tuesday or Thursday, given knowledge of items 1 and 2.

4. A is made aware of the promises by B and C, but cannot reach D.

Now A does not need to reach D as long as he trusts C to relay the history of the interactions. He can now see that the agents have not agreed on a time, but that if he can make Tuesday instead, there is a solution.

The lesson is that, in a world of incomplete information, trust can help you or harm you, but it's a gamble. The challenge in information science is to determine agreement based only on information that an agent can promise itself.

Promoting Cooperation by Incentive: Beneficial Outcome

Autonomous agents cannot be forced, but they can be voluntarily guided by incentives. Understanding what incentives motivate agents is not really a part of promise theory, per se; but, because there is a simple relationship between promises and mathematical games, it makes ample sense to adopt all that is known about the subject from noncooperative game theory. Making a bundle of promises may be considered a strategy in the game theoretical sense.

This means that if you want to promote cooperation, it's best to make promises that have perceived value to other agents. We'd better be careful though, because autonomous agents might value something quite unexpected—and not necessarily what we value ourselves. Offering money to a man without a parachute, on the way down from a plane, might not be an effective incentive. Value is in the eye of the beholder.

Some promise principles help to see how value arises:

Locality
> Avoid impositions, keep things close to you, and stay responsible.

Reciprocity
> Nurture a repeated relationship, think of what drives the economic motor of agent relationships.

Deal with uncertainties
> Have multiple contingencies for keeping promises. What will an agent do if a promise it relies on is not kept?

A television is a fragile system because it has no contingencies if a component, like the power supply, fails. An animal, on the other hand (or paw), has redundancy built in, and will not die from a single cell failure, or perhaps even the loss of a leg.

The Stability of Cooperation: What Axelrod Said

As hinted at in the last chapter, the science of cooperation has been studied at length using simple models of two-agent games, like the tug-of-war mentioned earlier. Political scientist Robert Axelrod, of the University of Michigan, explored the idea of games as models of cooperation in the 1970s. He asked: under what conditions will cooperative behaviour emerge in autonomous agents (i.e., without a God's-eye view of cooperation)?

Axelrod showed that the Nash equilibrium from economic game theory allowed cooperation to take place quite autonomously, based entirely on individual promises and assessments. He did not use the language of promises, but the intent was the same. Agents could perceive value in mutual promises completely asymmetrically as long as they showed consistency in their promises. Each agent could have its own subjective view on the scale of payment and currency; after all, value is in the eye of the beholder. It is well worth reading Axelrod's own account of these games, as there are several subtleties.[4]

The models showed that long-term value comes about when agents meet regularly. In a sense, they rehearse and reinforce their cooperation (as if rehearsing a piece on the piano) by reminding themselves of the value of it on a regular basis. This fits our everyday experience of getting the most out of a relationship when we practice, rehearse, revise, and repeat on a regular schedule. Scattered individuals who meet on an ad hoc basis will not form cooperative behaviour at all. Thus, the ongoing relationship may be essentially equated with the concept of lasting value. Put another way, it is not actions that represent lasting value, but rather the promise of repetition or persistently kept promises.

Interestingly, he also showed that stubborn strategies did not pay. Strategies in which agents behaved generously in an unconditional way, without putting preconditions ahead of their promises, led to the highest value outcomes for all parties as the cooperative relationship went on (Figure 5-9).

---

4 Robert Axelrod, *The Complexity of Cooperation: Agent-Based Models of Competition and Cooperation*, 1997.

Figure 5-9. Unconditional promises win out in the long run.

The Need to Be Needed: Reinterpreting an Innate Incentive?

Semantics play a large role in cooperation. The role of semantics is often under-estimated in decision models such as game theory, where it's assumed that all the intents and purposes are agreed to in advance. So while deciding about fixed choices is straightforward, there are few simple rules about interpretation of intent. Let's look at an interesting example of how agents can form their own interpretations of others' promises, reading in their own meanings, if you like.

The need to feel needed is one of the motivating factors that makes humans engage in their jobs. Perhaps this is even an innate quality in humans. We don't need warm, fuzzy feelings to see how this makes simple economic sense as a promise transaction. Pay attention to how we abstract away the humanity of a sit-uation in order to turn a situation into something systemic. This is how we turn vagaries of human behaviour into engineering, and it is what Promise Theory does quite well by having just enough traces of the human analogues left to make a plausible formalization.

Let's see what happens when we flip the signs of a promise to provide a ser-vice for payment (Figure 5-10). The counter-promise to use the service may be reinterpreted by saying that the service is needed or wanted by the other agent. Thus, if we flip the sign of the promise to give the service, this now translates into accepting the promise to be needed or wanted. In other words, providing a service plays the same role as needing to be needed, and it ends up next to the promise to receive actual payment.

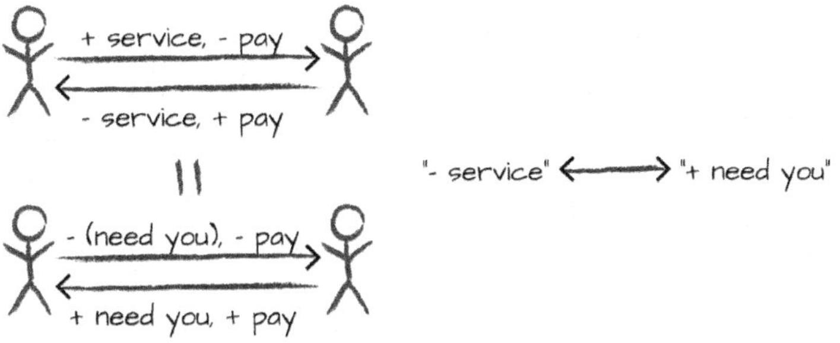

Figure 5-10. We can understand the need to be needed from the duality of +/- promises. For every +/- promise, there is a dual -/+ interpretation too.

Conversely, we could have started with the idea that needing to be needed was a promise. Requirements form use-promises (-). If we then abstract self into a generic agency of "the service," this becomes "need the service," and "use service from." Accepting the fact that your service is needed can straightforwardly, if mechanically, be interpreted as admitting that you will provide the service (without delving too deeply into the nuances of human wording). By flipping the polarity of complementary interpretations, it helps to unravel the mechanisms that lead to binding between agents.

Avoiding Conflicts of Interest

A conflict of interest is a situation where there are multiple promises and not all of them can be kept at the same time. How could we formulate promises so that conflicts of intent are minimized, and (should they occur) are obvious and fixable?

One way to avoid obvious difficulty is for each agent to divide up promises into types that do not interfere with one another. For example, I can promise to tie my shoelaces independently of promising to brush my teeth, but I can't promise to ride a bike independently of promising to ride a horse, because riding is an exclusive activity, making the promises interdependent.[5]

---

5 In mathematics, this is like looking for a spanning set of orthogonal vectors in a space. A change in X does not lead to a change in Y, so there is no conflict by promising either independently.

Figure 5-11. Conflicts arise immediately from impositions because the intent is not local and voluntary.

Impositions and obligations are a recipe for conflict (see Figure 5-11), because the source of intent is distributed over multiple agents. Promises can be made only about self, so they are always local and voluntary. Impositions can be refused, but this may also lead to confusion.

If obligations and requirements are made outside the location where they are to be implemented, the local implementors of that intent might not even know about them. This is is a recipe for distributed conflict.

Emergent Phenomena as Collective Equilibria: Forming Superagents

When we think of emergent behaviour, we conjure pictures of ant's nests or termite hills, flocks of birds, or shoals of fish (see Figure 5-12). However, most of the phenomena we rely on for our certain daily operations are emergent phenomena: the Internet, the economy, the weather, and so on. At some level, all behaviour of autonomous agents may be considered emergent. Unless explicit strong conditions are promised about every individual action, with a micromanaging level of detail, the behaviour cannot be deterministic.

As remarked previously, an emergent phenomenon is a mirage of semantics. An observer projects his own interpretation onto a phenomenon that appears to be organized, by assessing promises that are not really there. We imagine that the agencies we are observing must be making some kind of promise.

Figure 5-12. Cooperation by consensus or leadership.

Emergent phenomena result from the stable outcomes of agents working at the point of balance or equilibrium (see Figure 5-13).

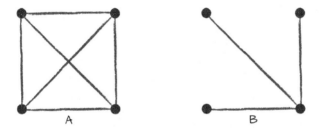

Figure 5-13. Two ways to equilibrate information/opinion: (a) swarm (everyone agrees with everyone individually as a society), (b) pilot leader (one leader makes an agreement with all subordinates, as a brain or glue for the collective).

Guiding the Outcome of Cooperation When It Is Emergent

Suppose we don't know all the promises a system runs on, but assume that it is operating at some equilibrium, with an emergent behaviour that we can observe. Could we still influence the behaviour and obtain a sense of control?

The starting point for this must be that the actual agents can be influenced, not merely the collective "superagent" (which has no channel for communicating because it is only a ghost of the others). Are they individually receptive to change? If they react to one another, then they might react to external influence too, thus one might piggyback on this channel.

If there is a leader in the group, it has short access to its subordinates, and is the natural place to effect change. If not, the process might take longer. There are two cases (see Figure 5-14).

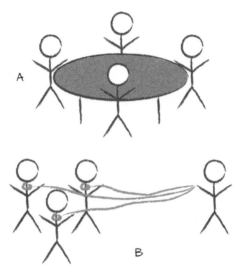

Figure 5-14. (a) and (b) again. This time (a) means sitting around a table and talking in a group, while (b) means dragging a team along with a single leader.

- In (a) there is no central decision point, but each agent has many links to equilibrate. The equilibration time might be longer with this system, but the result, once achieved, will be more robust. There is no single point that might fail.

- In (b) equilibration is faster, as there is a single point of consistency, and also of failure. It might be natural to choose that point as the leader, though there is nothing in theory that makes this necessary. This is a kind of leadership.

In a small team, you can have a strong leader and drag the others along by sheer effort. In a large team, the inertia of interacting with all of the subordinate agents will overwhelm the leader. If the leader agent loses its privileged position, then we revert to the default equilibration mechanism: autonomous, uncoordinated behaviour.

The structure of communications in these configurations suggests that change or adaptability, whether from within or without, favours small teams, or at least that the efficiency dwindles as teams get larger. Machines can be made to compensate for this by handling more communications, with greater brute force than humans can. Because of this, machines can handle larger groups without resorting to different tactics, but machines might not be able to keep the same promises as humans. This is one of the challenges of cybernetics and automation.

Although we might be able to influence the intention behind a cooperative group, we might not end up changing the behaviour if we ask it to do something that's unstable. How stable is the result with respect to behaviour (dynamics), interpretation (semantics), and cost (economics)?

One of the important lessons of Promise Theory is that semantics and intent are always subordinate to the dynamical possibilities of a situation. If something cannot actually be realized, it doesn't help to intend it furiously. Water will not flow uphill, no matter what the intent. With these caveats, one can still try to spread new actionable intentions to a group by starting somewhere and waiting for the changes to equilibrate through the cooperative channels that are already there. The more we understand the underlying promises, the easier it should be to crack the code.

Cooperation, Concensus, and Validation

Coordinating agencies in distributed systems by sharing information is the basis for many technologies. Software systems like CFEngine, Kubernetes, Zookeeper, and so on use algorithms such as Paxos, Raft, and variations on these, to promise consistency of data shared between agents. The cost of promising distributed consistency can be high, depending on exactly what is promised. The term *eventual consistency* is often used where agents in a system do not need a shared sense of time. In all cases, Promise Theory tells us that there are two approaches to equilibrating data: a peer-to-peer approach or a centralized master approach. In most cases a central master approach is used, and master backup agents exchange data as peers, making a hybrid solution. A central approach is limited to vertical scaling, while a peer-to-peer approach can scale horizontally.

Registration and security systems also use the two models for promising membership of a privileged group. In a *centralized* validation model, members (hotel clients, club members, authorized users, and so on) register themselves with a central agency, which in turn provides a service to validate according to its list. This is a trusted third-party model. The agents' public identity is effectively signed by the trusted central agency. In a *decentralized* model, each member carries personal credentials (a passport, a hotel key, a session identifier), which any agent of the system is empowered to verify at any time without contacting anyone else. It is everyone's individual responsibility to validate the credentials.

Stability of Intent: Erratic Behaviour?

Cooperation can be either between different agents, or with oneself over time. If an agent seems uncoordinated with respect to itself, an observer might label it erratic, or even uncooperative.[5] In a single agent, this could be dealt with as a problem in reliability. What about in a larger system?

Imagine a software company or service provider that changes its software promises over time. For example, a new version of a famous word processor changes the behaviour of a tool that you rely on. A website changes its layout, or some key functionality changes. These might not be actually broken promises, but are simply altered promises.

If the promises change too quickly, they are not useful tools for building expectation, and trust is stretched to a breaking point (see Figure 5-15). Such situations lessen the value of the promises. Users might begin to reevaluate whether they would trust an agent. In the example, software users want to trust the software or accept its promises, but a change throws their trust.

---

5 Interestingly, in Myers-Briggs personality typing, erratic or intuitive thinking versus sequential thinking is one of the distinctions that does lead to the misinterpretation of "artistic types" whose thoughts flit around without a perceivable target, as being erratic.

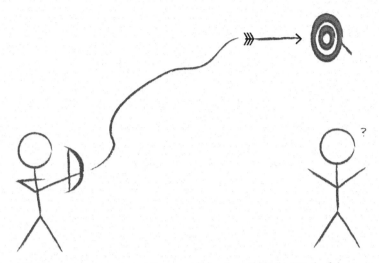

Figure 5-15. Converging to a target usually means behaving predictably! Lack of constant promises might lead to the perception of erratic behaviour.

Suppose an agent promises constant change, on the other hand. This is a possible way around the preceding issue. If promise users are promised constant change, then they can adjust their expectations accordingly. This is constancy at a meta-level. The point is that humans are creatures of habit or constant semantics. Changes in semantics lead to the reevaluation of trusted relationships, whether between humans directly, or by proxy through technology.

A way to avoid this is to maintain a principle of constancy of intent. This is actually the key to a philosophy that has grown up around so-called continuous delivery of services (see Chapter 8). One can promise change continuously, as long as the core semantics remain the same. New versions of reality for a product or service user must converge towards a stable set of intentions, and not be branching out into all kinds of possibilities.

This leads back to the matter of interpretation, however. Both human personalities and machine algorithms have different strategies for achieving constancy of intent. For example, searching for something in a store, or on the Internet, proposes a clear, intended target. The promise to search, however, can be approached in different ways. It might be implemented as a linear search (start at the beginning and work systematically through the list), or as a Monte Carlo approach, jumping to random locations and looking nearby. The latter approach sounds hopeless, but mathematically we know that this is by far the fastest approach to solving certain search problems.

Because perception often lies, agents have to be careful not to muddle desired outcomes with a preference for the modes of implementation.

When Being Not of One Mind Is an Advantage

Consensus and linear progressions are not always an advantage. There are methods in computation that rely on randomness, or unpredictable variation. These are called Monte Carlo methods, named after gambling methods, as random choices play a role in finding shortcuts. They are especially valuable in locating or searching for things.

This is just like the scene in the movies, where the protagonist says: "Let's split up. You search this way, I'll search that!"

Randomness and variation, so-called entropy, lie at the heart of solving so-called NP-hard problems, many of which have to do with decision-making and optimizing behaviours. We should not be too afraid of letting go of determinism and a sense of control.[5]

Human Error or Misplaced Intent?

Agreement in a group is called consensus. There does not need to be consensus in order for cooperative behaviour to come about, but there does need to be a sufficient mutual understanding of the meaning of promises.

In some systems, a common view comes about slowly by painstaking equilibration of intent. In other cases, agents will elect to follow some guiding star that short-circuits the process. The analogues in politics include dictators and democracies. Dictatorship has some efficiency about it, but many feel it is dehumanizing. It works very well when the agents who follow the leader do not have a need for individual freedom (e.g., parts in a machine).

Individuality can be a burden if it stands in the way of cooperation. However, the way we scale large industrial efforts by brute human force has led up to the model of trying to build machines from human parts. If people can give up their individuality (but not their humanity), and act as one mind, rather than one body, engineering would be a simple optimization problem. Consider it a goal of Promise Theory to depersonalize matters so that this is not an emotional decision.

---

5 I wrote about this in detail in my book, *In Search of Certainty: The Science of Our Information Infrastructure*.

By putting humans into machine-like scenarios, we often assert that humans are to blame for errors and erratic behaviours, because we expect machine-like behaviours. From a promise viewpoint, we see that one cannot make promises of machine-like behaviour on behalf of humans. If a user of promises does not rate the performance of another agent highly, it is up to that user to find a more compatible agent. Thus, instead of saying that people are the problem, we can say that semantics are the problem.

Semantics come from people too, but from those who observe and judge the outcomes of promised situations. If we expect something that was not promised, the desire for blame is the emotional response, and the search for a replacement is the pragmatic response.

Organization: Centralization Versus Decentralization

The argument for centralizing or decentralizing control is one of those ongoing debates in every area of engineering and design. We gravitate towards centralized models of control because they are familiar and easy to understand.

I like to call a centralized architecture a brain model (i.e., one in which there is a centralized controller that reaches out to a number of sensors and actuators through a network with the intent to control it). See Figure 5-16.

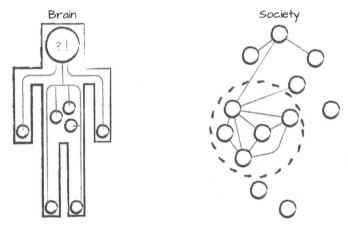

Figure 5-16. Central brains and distributed societies. A brainy dictator can be more agile than the slow consensus of a society, but is less robust.

Obviously, this is how brains are positioned (though not how they work internally); the brain is localized as a logically centralized controller, and the nervous system connects it to the rest of the body for sending and receiving pulses of communication. Not all of the body's systems are managed in this way, of course, but the intentional aspects of our behaviour are.

A brain model is a signalling model. Signals are transmitted from a common command-and-control centre out to the provinces of an organism, and messages are returned to allow feedback. We are so familiar with this approach to controlling systems that we nearly always use it as the model of control. We see it in vertebrates; we use it to try to force-govern societies, based on police or military power; and we see it in companies. Most of management thinking revolves around a hierarchy of controllers. The advantage of this model is that we can all understand it. After all, we live it every day. But there is one problem: it doesn't scale favourably to a large size.

The alternative to a brain model is what I'll call a society model. I imagine a number of autonomous parts that are loosely coupled, without a single central controller. There can be cooperation between the parts (e.g., institutions or departments, communities or towns, depending on whether the clustering is logical or geographical). There are even places where certain information gets centralized (e.g., libraries, governing watchdogs, etc.), but the parts are capable of surviving independently and even reconfiguring without a central authority.

Societies can easily grow to a larger scale brain models because work can be shared between several agents which interact weakly at the edges, trading or exchanging information. If one connection to a service fails, the service does not necessarily become cut off from the rest, and it has sufficient autonomy to reconfigure and adapt. There is no need for a path from every part of the system to a single God-like location, which then has to cope with the load of processing and decision-making by sheer brute force.

The autonomous agent concept in Promise Theory allows us to recognize the limitations of not having information in a single place. By bringing together information into one place, a centralized system, like a brain, can make decisions that require analysis more consistently since only a single point of calibration is needed. From a promise perspective, a brain is a single agent that defines a role. It must be in possession of all the knowledge, and it must trust that knowledge in order to use it decisively. If these things are promised, and all other agents subordinate to the brain, this can be an effective model of cooperation. Most hierarchical organizations follow this model.

A brain *service*, whether centralized or embedded in a society, promises to handle impositions thrust upon it by sensors, and to respond to actuators by returning its own impositions. It's a pushy model. It also promises to process and make decisions; thus any brain will benefit from speed and processing power. Any agent can handle up to a certain maximum capacity of impositions per second before becoming oversubscribed. Thus every agent is a bottleneck to handling impositions. Horizontal expansion (like a society) by parallelization handles this in a scale-free manner. Vertical expansion (like a central brain) has to keep throwing brute force, capacity, and speed at the problem. Moore's law notwithstanding, this probably has limits.

Focused Interventions or Sweeping Policies?

The brain idea is a nice analogy, but it might be making you think too much about humans again, so let's think about another example.

Flourescent lightbulbs are an interesting case of a cooperative system of agents (i.e., gaseous atoms that emit light together by an avalanche effect when stimulated electrically). You've probably seen two kinds of these: long strip lights, and short, folded bulb replacements.

Quick-start tubes have starter circuits that dump a quick surge of electrical current through the gas in the tube to create a sudden avalanche effect that lights up the whole tube in one go. Such tubes use a lot of energy to get started, but they start quickly. Most of the energy is used in switching them on. Once they are running, they use very little energy. Their (conditional) promise is to give off a strong light at low cost *if* you leave them switched on for long periods of time.

Newer "energy-saving" lightbulbs make a similar promise, but unconditionally. They don't use quick-start capacitors, so they take a long time to warm up. This uses a lot less energy during startup, but the atoms take longer to reach a consensus and join the cooperative party. Once all the atoms have been reached, the light is just as bright and behaves in the same way as the older tubes.

The starter circuit in the first kind of tube acts as a central brain, imposing a consensus onto the atoms by brute force. Once the light is working, it has no value anymore, and the atoms run away with the process quite autonomously. Sometimes a brief intervention can shift from one stable state to another, without carrying the burden constantly.

For humans, it's a bit like that when we are rehearsing something. Our brains as we imagine them really means our neocortex or logical brain. If we are learning a new piece on the piano, we need to use that intervention brain. But once we've practiced enough, the routine gets consigned to what we like to call *muscle memory* (the limbic system), which is much cheaper, and we no longer need to think about the process anymore. We might try to cram knowledge into our brains to kickstart the process, but it only gets cheap to maintain with continuity.

When we can replace impositions with stable promises, interventions can be replaced by ongoing policies. The result is cheaper and longer lasting. It can be just as agile if the policy is one of continuous change.

Societies and Functional Roles

The alterative to the central brain approach is to allow agents to cooperate individually. In the extreme case, this adds a lot of peer-to-peer communication to the picture, but it still allows agents to develop specializations and work on behalf of one another cooperatively.

Specialization means regions of different agency, with benefits such as focused learning, and so on. Agents can save costs by focusing on a single discipline. In Promise Theory, specialists should be understood as separate agents, each of which promises to know how to do its job. Those regions could be decentralized, as in societal institutions, or they could be specialized regions of a central brain (as in Washington DC or the European parliament). The advantage of decentralization is that there are fewer bottlenecks that limit the growth of the system. The disadvantage is that agents are not subordinated uniquely to one agency, so control is harder to perceive, and slower to equilibrate. Thus, decentralized systems exhibit scalability without brute force, at the cost of being harder to comprehend and slower to change.

A centralized brain makes it easier (and faster) for these institutional regions to share data, assuming they promise to do so, but it doesn't place any limits on possibility. Only observation and correlation (calibration) require aggregation of information in a single *central* location.

Relationships: What Dunbar Said

Every promise binding is the basis for a relationship. Robert Axelrod showed, using game theory, that when such relationships plan for long-term gains, they become stable and mutually beneficial to the parties involved. An interesting counterpoint to that observation comes from realizing that relationships cost effort to maintain.

Psychologist Robin Dunbar discovered an important limitation of relationships from an anthropological perspective while studying the brain sizes of humans and other primates. He discovered that the modern (neocortical) brain size in primates limits how many relationships we can keep going at the same time. Moreover, the closer or more intimately we revisit our relationships, the fewer we can maintain, because a close relationship costs more to maintain. This has to play a role in the economics of cooperation. In other words, relationships cost, and the level of attention limits how many we can maintain. This means that there is a limit to the number of promises we can keep. Each agent has finite resources.

We seem to have a certain number of *slots* we can use for different levels of repetitive cost. Human brains can manage around 5 intimate relationships, around 15 in a family-like group, about 30 to 40 in a tribal or departmental working relationship, and 100 to 150 general acquaintances. Whatever semantics we associate with a group (i.e., whether we consider someone close a lover or a bitter enemy), family, or team—is the level of cognitive processing, or intimacy, that limits the number we can cope with. Once again, dynamics trump semantics.

We can now ask, what does this say about other kinds of relationships, with work processes, tools, or machinery? Cooperation is a promise we cannot take lightly.

Some Exercises

1. Think of daily activities where you believe you are in full control, like driving a car, making dinner, typing on your computer, giving orders at work, etc. Now try to think of the agents you rely on in these activities (car engine, tyres, cooker, coworkers, etc.) and rethink these cases as cooperative systems. What promises do the agencies you rely on make to you? What would happen if they didn't keep their promises?

2. Compare so-called IT orchestration systems (scheduling and coordinating IT changes) that work by imposition (e.g., remote execution frameworks, network shells, push-based notification, etc.), with those that work by promising to coordinate (e.g., policy consistency frameworks with shared data). Compare the availability and robustness of the coordination by thinking about what happens if the promises they rely on are not kept.

3. Sketch out the promises and compare peer-to-peer systems (e.g., Skype, bit-torrent, OSPF, BGP, CFEngine, etc.), with *follow the leader* systems using directory services or control databases (e.g., etcd, consul, zookeeper,

openvswitch, CFEngine, etc.). What is the origin of control in these two approaches to collaboration?

4. In IT product delivery, the concept of DevOps refers to the promises made between software developers and operations or system administrators that enable smooth delivery of software from intended design to actual consumption by a user. Think of a software example, and document the agencies and their promises in such a delivery. You should include, at least, developers, operations engineers, and the end user.

6

Engineering Component Systems

Tidiness is next to Godliness, or so goes the mantra of the obsessive compulsive. The partially decentralized society model of cooperation proves to be an important pattern when designing cooperative systems, but it leads to apparent complexity, too. An apparent way around this is to find a middle ground by dividing it up into specialized components.

During the 1800s, Western culture became particularly obsessed with the need to categorize things and separate them tidily into boxes. One reason might be that we cannot hold many things in our minds because of our limited Dunbar slots. Whatever the reason, our cultural aesthetic is for putting things tidily into boxes, and arranging shelves neatly.

Meanwhile, jungles and ecosystems stubbornly refuse to be patterned in this oversimplistic way. Nature selected tangled webs as its strategy for stable survival, not carefully organized rows and columns, or taxonomic trees of partitioned species. Those organizational structures are all human designs.

There are plenty of reasons why tidiness would not be a successful strategy for keeping promises. The complexity of bonding and maintaining an interactive relationship across boundaries is the understated price we pay for a tidy separation of concerns, when pieces cannot really do without one another.

Yet, building things from replicable patterns (like cells) is exactly what nature does. So the idea of making components with different functional categories is not foreign to nature. Where does the balance lie? Let's see what light promises can shed on this matter.

Reasoning with Cause

Engineering is based on a model of cause and effect. If we can identify a property or phenomenon X, such that it reliably implies phenomenon Y under certain circumstances, then we can use it to keep promises that make a functional world. Indeed, if we can promise these properties, then we can engineer with some certainty.

For example, if an agent promises to use a service X in order to keep a promise of its own Y, then we could infer that promise Y is fragile to the loss of service X. These are chains of prerequisite dependence (see Figure 6-1).

Figure 6-1. Reasoning leads to branching processes that fan out into many possibilities and decrease certainty. The result can be as fragile as a house of cards.

Philosophers get into a muddle over what causation means, but engineers are pragmatic. We care less about whether we can argue precisely what caused an effect than we care about whether there is a possibility that an effect we rely on might go away. We manage such concerns by thinking about arranging key promises to dominate outcomes, in isolation from interfering effects. This is not quite the same thing as the "separation of concerns" often discussed in IT. Ironically, this usually means that if we need to couple systems together, we make as many of those couplings as possible *weak*, to minimize the channels of causal influence.

Componentization: Divide and Build!

The design of functional systems from components is a natural topic to consider from the viewpoint of autonomous agents and their promises. How will we break down a problem into components, and how do we put together new and unplanned systems from a preexisting set of parts? Indeed, the concept of autonomous agents exists for precisely this purpose.

Decomposing systems into components is not *necessary* for systems to work (an alternative with similar cost-benefit is the use of repeatable patterns during construction of a singular entity), but it is often desirable for economic reasons.

A component design is really a commoditization of a reusable pattern, and the economics of component design are the same as the economics of mass production.

The electronics industry is a straightforward and well-known example of component design and use. There we have seen how the first components—resistors, inductors, capacitors, and transistors—were manufactured as ranges of separate atomic entities, each making a variety of promises about its properties. Later, as miniaturization took hold, many of these were packaged into *chips* that were more convenient, but less atomic, components. This has further led to an evolution of the way in which devices are manufactured and repaired. It is more common now to replace an entire integrated unit than to solder in a new capacitor, for example.

An analogy with medicine would be to favour transplanting whole organs rather than repairing existing ones.

What Do We Mean by Components?

Being more formal about what we mean by promises allows us to understand other definitions that build on them. Components are a good example of how to use the agent concept flexibly to reason about designs.

A component is an entity that behaves like an agent and makes a number of promises to other agents, within the context of a system. It could be represented as a bundle of promises emanating from a localized place. Components play a role within the scope of a larger system. For weakly coupled systems, components can be called standalone.

A standalone or independent component is an agent that makes only unconditional promises. For example, a candle stands alone, but is part of a room. In strongly coupled systems or subsystems, components are integral parts, embedded in a larger whole. A dependent (or embedded) component is an agent that makes one or more conditional promises, such as flour or sugar in a cake (see Figure 6-2).

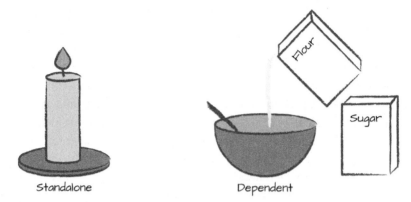

Figure 6-2. Components can be standalone, without dependencies, or dependent.

What Systemic Promises Should Components Keep?

In addition to the functional promises that components try to keep, there are certain issues of design that would tend to make us call an agent a component of a larger system. Typical promises that components would be designed to keep could include:

- To be replaceable or upgradable
- To be reusable, interchangeable, or compatible
- To behave predictably
- To be (maximally) self-contained, or avoid depending on other components to keep their promises

When an object is a component, it has become separated from the source of its intent. It is *another brick in the wall.*

Can Agents Themselves Have Components? (Superagents)

What about the internal structure of agents in the promises? Can they have components? The answer depends on the level of detail to which we want to decompose an object and talk about its promises. Clearly, components can have as much private, internal structure as we like—that is a matter of design choice.

For example, we might consider a cake to be a component in a supermarket inventory. This makes certain promises like chocolate flavour, nut-free, low calorie, and so on. The cake has a list of ingredients or components too, like flour and sugar. The flour might promise to be whole grain, and the sugar might promise to be brown sugar. The definition of agents is a modelling choice.

When we aggregate agents into a new compound agency, I'll use the term *superagent*.

Component Design and Roles

One simple structure for promise patterns is to map components onto roles. A component is simply a collection of one or more agents that forms a role, either by association or cooperation. Once embedded within a larger system, these roles can become appointed too, through the binding relationships with users and providers. Table 6-1 illustrates some example components and their roles in some common systems.

Table 6-1. Examples of system components

System	Component	Role
Television	Integrated circuit	Amplifier
Pharmacy	Pill	Sedative
Patient	Intravenous drug	Antibiotic
Vertebrate	Bone	Skeleton
Cart	Wheel	Mobility enabler
Playlist	Song by artist	Soft jazz interlude

Components Need to Be Assembled

A collection of components does not automatically become a system, unless perhaps it possesses *swarm intelligence*, like a flock of birds. Anyone who has been to IKEA knows that tables and chairs do not spontaneously self-assemble.

To complete a system composed of components, agents need to bind their matching promises together. Think of flat-packed furniture from IKEA, and you find clips, parts that plug into receptors, or screws that meet holes. These are effectively (+) and (-) promises made by the parts that say "I will bind to this kind of receptor" (see Figure 6-3).

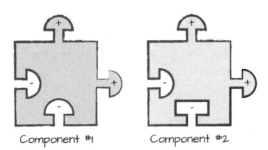

Figure 6-3. Promises that give something (+), and promises that accept something (-), match in order to form a binding, much like a jigsaw puzzle.

In biology, there is the concept of receptors, too. Molecular receptors on cells (MHC) identify cells' signatures to proteins that would bind to them. Viruses that have the proper parts to plug into receptors, but which subvert the normal function of the cell, can pervert the cell's normal behaviour. Humans, making a semantic assessment, view this as a sickness because the cell is not behaving according to what they consider to be its intended purpose. Of course, evolution is not in the business of intent; it merely makes things that survive. We humans, on the other hand, project the hand of intent into everything.

The relationships formed between components need to be stable if the larger system is to remain stable.

Conduits and Pipes

A set of promises that is very familiar from the Unix operating system is the input/output channels called *stdin* (-), *stdout* (+), and *stderr* (+). These three channels of data are promised by every process (agent) running on a Unix-like operating system today. Processes can be combined as components to cooperate towards a larger purpose by binding these channels together using *pipes*. In each case, a pipe binds a (+) output source to a (-) input channel.

Fragile Promises in Component Design

Building an appliance on components that make exclusive promises (i.e., promises that can be kept only for a limited number of users) is a fragile strategy. Trying to design for the avoidance of such conflicts is a good idea; however, one often has incomplete information about how components will be used, making this impossible to predict. This is one of the flaws in top-down design.

Some components contend for their dependencies. Components that make conditional promises, where the condition must be satisfied by only one exclusive promise from another component, may be called *contentious* or *competitive*. Multiple agents contend with one another to satisfy the the condition, but only one agent can do so. For example, you can only plug one appliance into a power socket at a time. Only one patient can swallow a pill at a time, thus a pill is a contentious agent that promises relief if taken.

Designing with contentious components can sometimes save on costs, but can lead to bottlenecks and resource issues in continuous system operation. Contentious promises are therefore fragile.

- For example, consider an engine that promises to run only if it gets a special kind of fuel would be risky. What if the fuel becomes scarce (i.e., it cannot be promised)?

- Multiple electrical appliances connected to the same power line contend for the promise of electrical power. If the maximum rating is a promise of, say, 10 Amperes, multiple appliances requiring a high current could easily exceed this.

- A similar example can be made with traffic. Cars could be called contentious components of traffic, as they contend for the limited road and petrol/gas pumps at fueling stations.

- Software applications running on a shared database or server have to contend for availability and capacity.

Contention in the Data Center

Before cloud services became widely available, IT applications and services were run on dedicated servers that would promise availability and response times. Those promises were necessarily limited by finite resources, and users would contend to have their promises kept. Today, the challenge lies in arranging additional coooperative promises between servers, so that the business application promises can be kept without hard limits. This is often called *elastic scaling*, and it is a key enabler for *cloud computing*.

The examples reveal the effect of imperfect information during component design. The designer of an appliance cannot know the availability of dependencies when designing an isolated component, which begs the question: should one try to design components without the context of their use? The alternative is to allow components to emerge through experience, and abstract them out of their contexts by observing a common pattern.

We make risky choices usually to minimize costs, given the probability of needing to deliver on a promise of a resource. The risk comes from the fact that contention between promises is closely related to single points of failure in coordination and calibration. Contention leads to fragility.

Reusability of Components

If we are able to partition systems into components that make well-understood promises, then it's natural to suppose that some of these promises will be useful is more than one scenario. Then we can imagine making components of general utility—reusable components.

Reusability is about being able to take a component that promises to work in one scenario and use it in another. We achieve this when we take an agent and insert it into another system of agents, whose use-promises match our component's promises.

Any agent or agency can be reusable, so don't think just about electronic components, flour and sugar, and so on. Think also about organizations, accounts departments, human beings that promise skills, and even movies. For instance, a knife is a component that can be used in many different scenarios for cutting. It doesn't matter if it is used to cut bread or cheese, or to perform surgery. Electrical power offers a promise that can be used by a large number of other components, so we may call that reusable. Reusability means that a component makes a promise that can be accepted by and bind to many other agents' use-promises (see Figure 6-4).

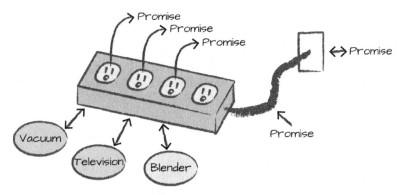

Figure 6-4. Reusability of a power adapter as a component that makes promises to share electric current from a plug to a number of sockets.

Formally, a component cannot be intrinsically reusable, but it can be reusable relative to some other components within its field of use. Then we can say that a component is reusable if its promised properties meet or exceed the use-promises (requirements) of every environment in which it is needed.

Reusable Resources in IT

Computer systems are all about promising information resources to consumers. Nearly every basic resource in a computer system may be thought of as a pool of autonomous agents that make promises to users. The reusable agents bind to users to provide CPU time slices, memory pages, network addresses, network packets, and so on. Systems cooperate by following standards for these agencies: each resource is composed of reusable agencies that have the same basic size, shape, and behaviour. This means that they can be used and reused generically.

Interchangeability of Components

Two components might be called interchangeable, relative to an observer, if every promise made by the first component to the observer is also made identically by the second, and vice versa.

When components are changed, or revised, the local properties of the resulting system could change. This might further affect the promises of the entire system, as perceived by a user, assuming that the promise bindings allow it. In continuous delivery systems, changes can be made at any time as long as the semantics are constant.

If the semantics of the components change, either the total composite system has to change its promises, or a total revision of the design might be needed to maintain the same promises of the total system. Interchangeable components promise that this will not happen (see Figure 6-5).

Figure 6-5. Interchangeability means that components have to make exactly the same promises. These two power strips are not interchangeable.

A knife can be interchanged with an identical new knife in a restaurant without changing the function, even if one has a wooden handle and the other, a plastic one. A family pet probably can't be interchanged with another family pet without changing the total family system.

Compatibility of Components

Compatibility of components is a weaker condition than interchangeability. Two components may be called compatible if one forms the same set of promise bindings with an agent as the second, but the details of the promises might not be identical in every aspect. A component might simply be "good enough" to be fit for the purpose.

Compatibility means that all the essential promises are in place. If components are compatible, it is possible for them to bind to the same contexts, even if the precise promises are not maintained at the same levels (see Figure 6-6).

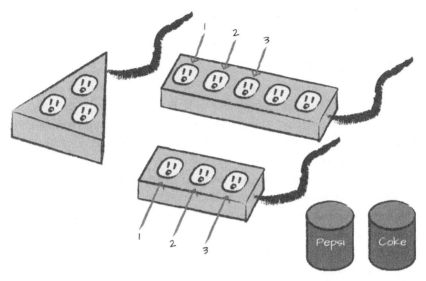

Figure 6-6. Compatibility means that a replacement will do the job without all the promises being identical. This is up the the the user of the promises to judge.

British power plugs are not interchangeable or compatible with the power sockets in America or the rest of Europe because they do not make complementary promises. Similarly, we can say that British and American power plugs are not interchangeable. British power plugs are somewhat over-engineered for robustness and safety, with individual fuses to isolate damaged equipment.

Conversely, there might be cases where it doesn't matter which of a number of alternative components is chosen—the promises made are unspecific and the minor differences in how promises are kept do not affect a larger outcome. In other scenarios, it could matter explicitly. Imagine two brands of chocolate cake at the supermarket. These offerings can be considered components in a larger network of promises. How do we select or design these components so that other promises can be kept?

- *Doesn't matter*: You would normally choose a cheap brand of cake, but it is temporarily unavailable, so you buy the more expensive premium version.

- *Matters*: One of the cakes contains nuts that you are allergic to, so it does not fulfill your needs.

If the promise made by the cake is too unspecific for its consumer, there can be a mismatch between expectation and service.

Backward Compatibility

Replacement components are often said to require backward compatibility, meaning that a replacement component will not undermine the promises made by an existing system. In fact, if one wants status quo, the correct term should be interchangeability, as a new component might be compatible but still not function in the same way.

When repairing devices, we are tempted to replace components with new ones that are almost the same, but this can lead to problems, even if the new components are *better* in relation to their own promises. For example, the promise of increased power in a new engine for a plane might lead to an imbalance in the engines, making handling difficult. Similarly, changing one tyre of a car might cause the car to pull in one direction.

Making the same kinds of promises as an older component is a necessary condition for interchangeability, but it is not sufficient to guarantee no change in the total design. We need identical promises, no more and no less, else there is the possibility that new promises introduced into a component will conflict with the total system in such a way as to be misaligned with the goals of the total design.

Diesel fuel makes many of the same promises as petrol or gasoline, but these fuels are not interchangeable in current engines. A new super-brand of fuel might promise better performance, but might wear out the engine more quickly. The insertion of new output transistors with better specification into a particular hi-fi amplifier actually improves the sound quality of the device. The transistors cannot be considered interchangeable, even though there is an improvement, because the promises they make are not the same, and the total system is affected. Now the older system is weaker and cannot be considered an adequate replacement for the new one.

Promises for Realism in Design

A promise viewpoint of a component system shifts attention away from dreams of architecture to focus on practical purpose. Promised collaboration must be constructed from the bottom up (i.e., from the promises we know the agents on the ground can keep, rather than the promises we would ideally like them to make). Because this bases cooperation on what we know, rather than what we wish for, it is a dose of realism. It might not be possible to promise the final purpose exactly as we'd like, but it's surely better to know that, than to believe in a top-down lie.

Upgrading and Regression Testing of Components

When upgrading components that are not identical, a possibility is to design in a compatibility mode such that no new promises are added when they are used in this way. This allows component promises to remain interchangeable and expectations to be maintained. Downgrading can also be compatible but not interchangeable.

Figure 6-7. A regression test involves assessing whether component promises are still kept after changing the component. Does today's piece of cake taste as good as yesterday's piece?

A regression test is a trip wire or probe that makes a promise (-) to assess a service promise made by some software. The same promise is made to every agent promising a different version of the service promise. The ability to detect faults during testing depends on both what is promised (+) and what is used (-) by the test-agent.

Designing Promises for a Market

Imagine we have a number of components that make similar promises (e.g., screws, power sockets, servers, and software products). If the promises are identical, then the components are identical, and it clearly doesn't matter which component we use. However, if the promises are generic and vague, there is a high level of uncertainty in forming expectations about the behaviour of the components.

For example, suppose a car rental company promises us a vehicle. It could give us a small model, a large model, a new model, a clapped-out wreck, or even a motorbike. It could be German, Japanese, American, etc. Clearly the promise of "some kind of vehicle" is not sufficiently specific for a user to necessarily form useful expectations.

Similarly, in a restaurant, it says "meat and vegetables" on the menu. Does this mean a medium-rare beef steak with buttered carrots and green beans, or baked rat with fries?

The potential for a mismatch of expectation steers how components should design their interfaces for consumers and systems with similar promises. It is often desirable for an agent consuming promises to have a simple point of contact (sometimes called a *frontend*) that gives them a point of one-stop shopping. This has both advantages and disadvantages to the user, as interchangeability of the backend promises is not assured.

Law of the Lowest Common Denominator

If a promiser makes a *lowest common denominator* promise, it is easy for users of the promise to consume (i.e., to understand and accept), but the vagueness of the promise makes it harder to trust in a desired outcome.

For example, supermarkets often rebrand their goods with generic labels like *mega-store beans* or *super-saver ice cream*. The lack of choice makes it easy for the user to choose, but it also means that the user doesn't know what she is getting. Often in these cases, the promise given is implicitly one of a minimum level of quality.

In computing, a service provider offers a "SQL database" service. There are many components that offer this service, with very different implementations. PostgreSQL, MySQL, MSSQL, Oracle, and several others all claim to promise an SQL database. However, the detailed promises are very different from one another so that the components are not interchangeable. Writing software using a common interface to these databases thus leads to using only the most basic common features.

> *The law of the lowest common denominator. When a promise-giving component makes a generic promise interface to multiple components, it is forced to promise the least common denominator or minimal common functionality. Thus, generic interfaces lead to low certainty of outcome.*

The user of a promise is both the driver and the filter to decide what must be satisfied (i.e., the agent's *requirements*). This is how we paraphrase the idea that "the customer is always right" in terms of promises. If the user promises to use any *meat-and-vegetables* food promise by a caterer, he will doubtless end up with something of rather low quality, but if he promises to use only "seared filet, salted, no pepper," the provider will have to promise to deliver on that, else the user would not accept it to form a promise binding.

Imposing Requirements: False Expectations

When designing or productizing components for consumers, it's much more common to use the language of imposing requirements. Use-promises or impositions about specifications play equivalent roles in setting user expectations for promised outcomes. Both create a sense of obligation.

The problem is clear. If we try to start with user expectations, there is no reason why we might be able to fulfill them by putting together available components and resources. Only the component agents know what they can promise.

Cooperation is much more likely if intent is not imposed on individuals, especially when they are humans. Starting with what has been promised makes a lot more sense when agents only promise their own capabilities. Thus, if one can engineer voluntary cooperation by incentive, it is easier to trust the outcome of the promise.

This lesson has been seen in many cooperative scenarios, for example, where one group "throws a job over the wall" to another ("Catch!") and expects it to be taken care of (see Figure 6-8).[5]

---

5 In IT, the DevOps movement came about in this way as software developers threw their latest creations over the proverbial wall to operations engineers to run in production.

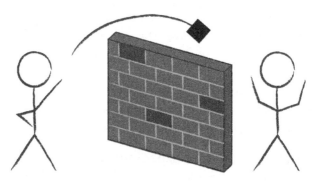

Figure 6-8. Throwing impositions over the wall is unreliable. A promise handshake gives better assurances.

If one trades this interaction for a continuous promise relationship, trust grows on both sides.

Component Choices That You Can't Go Back On

Selecting one particular component from a collection has long-term consequences for component use and design if one selects a noninterchangeable component. The differences that are specific to its promises then lead the system along a path that moves farther away from the alternatives because other promises will come to rely on this choice through dependencies.

Choosing to use a fuel type to power a car (e.g., using a car that makes a diesel rather than a petrol/gasoline promise, has irreversible consequences for further use of that component). Choosing the manufacturing material for an aircraft, or the building site for a hotel, has irreversible consequences for their future use. Another example is the side of the road that countries drive on. Historians believe that driving on the lefthand side goes back to ancient Rome, and that this was the norm until Napolean created deliberate contention in Europe. Today, driving on the right is the dominant promise, but countries like the UK are locked into the opposite promise by the sheer cost of changing.[5] A similar argument could be made about the use of metric and imperial measures across the world.[6]

---

5 Sweden made the change from driving on the left to the right overnight, avoiding accidents by arranging a campaign of staying at home to watch television.

6 The UK has made limited efforts to change to metric units by showing both units in some cases, but this has had little real impact.

Choosing to use one political party has few irreversible consequences, as it is unlikely that any other promises by the agent making the choice would depend on this choice.

Stuck with Networking

The history of computer networking is a study in being paralyzed by choices from the past. But it is also an example of how open cooperation finally wins out over closed competition. Many proprietary technologies have been introduced by computer manufacturers over the years. Having promised networking, making these choices has locked these systems into supporting them for years to come.

The Internet Protocol suite (IPv4) was the first standard to achieve real success, and by its many components it represents the dominant set of promises made by networking systems around the world today. However, its limitations make for a contentious set of promises, as well as a number of design flaws. Newer alternatives (e.g., IPv6) are in partial use (somewhat like the metric system is used in the UK and US); however, the world is stuck on IPv4 until something encourages large-scale adoption of a system that can coexist with IPv4 and eventually succeed it.[5]

The Art of Versioning

When we develop a tool or service, we release versions of these to the world. Now we have to ask, do version changes and upgrades keep the same promises as before? If not, is it the same product?

Consider Figure 6-9, which shows how a single promise agent can depend on a number of other agents. If the horizontal stacking represents components in a design, and vertical stacking indicates different versions of the same component, then each agent would be a replaceable and upgradable part.

---

5 This illustrates that when you issue is communication itself; it makes little sense to be stubborn about the language you speak, even if the language is imperfect.

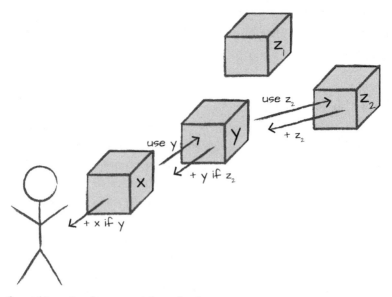

Figure 6-9. A hierarchy of component dependencies.

In a system with multiple cross-dependencies, different versions of one component may depend on different versions of others. How may we be certain to keep consistent promises throughout a total system made of many such dependencies, given that any of the components can be reused multiple times, and may be interchanged for another during the course of a repair or upgrade? There is a growth of combinatorial complexity, which can lead to collapse by information overload as we exceed the Dunbar slots we have at our disposal.[5]

Consider the component arrangement in Figure 6-10, showing a component X that relies on another component Y, which in turn relies on component Z. The components exist in multiple versions, and the conditional promises made by X and Y specifically refer to these versions, as they must in order to be certain of what detailed promise is being kept.

---

5 See my book, *In Search of Certainty*, for a discussion of how Dunbar's number applies to technology.

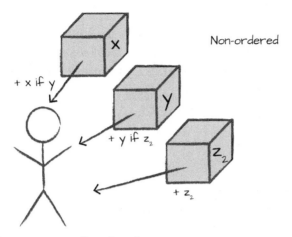

Figure 6-10. A flat arrangement of interdependent components.

This situation is fragile if components Y and Z are altered in some way. There is no guarantee that X can continue to promise the same as before, thus its promise to its users is conditional on a given version of the components that it relies on, and each change to a component should be named differently to distinguish among these versions.

To avoid this problem, we can make a number of rules that guide the design of components.

If components promise dependency usage in a version-specific way, supporting components can coexist without contention. Promises by one component to use another can avoid being broken by referring to the specific versions that quench their promises-to-use. This avoids the risk of later invalidation of the promises by the component as the dependency versions evolve.

Non-version-specific promises are simpler to make and maintain, but they do not live in their own branch of reality, and thus they cannot simultaneously coexist. This is why multiple versions must be handled such that they can coexist without confusion or conflict. This is the *many worlds* issue.

Versioning takes care of the matter of component evolution and improvement in the presence of dependency. The next issue is what happens if a component is used multiple times within the same design. Can this lead to conflicts? There are now two issues surrounded by repeated promises:

- If multiple components, with possibly several versions, make completely identical promises, this presents no problem, as identical promises are idempotent, meaning that they lead to compatible outcomes.

- Incompatible, also called exclusive, promises prevent the reuse of components.

Note

Any component that can be used multiple times, for different purposes, within the same system, must be able to exist alongside other versions of the component and patterns of usage. Component versions that collaborate to avoid making conflicting promises across versions can more easily coexist.

The unique naming of components is a simple way to avoid some of these problems. We will describe this in the next section.

Version Branching and Conflict Avoidance

The popular version-control software *git* is a good example of how agents can coexist without interference. Data stored in git may be used multiple times, and adopted and evolved for different purposes using so-called *branches* and *forks*. Each branch or fork becomes an independent agent that lives autonomously without conflict. These agents can promise cooperation with other branch/fork agents that promise to cooperate, if one promises to make its data available, and the other promises to use (pull) and merge. By breaking changes (commits) into independent promises (diffs), one minimizes the likelihood of contention between the promises. By this design, no branch can introduce a conflict for another unless the latter has voluntarily chosen to accept such a conflict.

Names and Identifiers for "Branding" Component Promises

A simple matter like naming turns out to play an important role. A name is a promise that can imply many other promises in a given cultural arena. For example, if we promise someone a car, currently at least this would imply a promise of wheels.

What attributes qualify as names? Names do not have to be words. A name could be a shape. A cup does not need a name for us to recognize it. Components need to promise their function somehow, with some representation that users will recognize. Naming, in its broadest sense, allows components to be recognizable and distinguishable for reuse. Recognition may occur through shape, texture, or any form of sensual signalling.

In marketing, this kind of naming is often called *branding*. The concept of branding goes back to identifying marks burnt onto livestock. In marketing, branding looks at many aspects of the psychology of naming, as well as how to attract the attention of onlookers to make certain components more attractive to users than others.

It makes sense that bundles of promises make naming agreements within a system, according to their functional role, allowing components to be:

- Quickly recognizable for use

- Distinguishable from other components

- Built from cultural or instinctive knowledge

Because an agent cannot impose its name on another agent, nor can it know how another agent refers to it, naming conventions have to be common knowledge within a collaborative subsystem. Establishing and trusting names is one of the fundamental challenges in systems of agents. This issue mirrors the acceptance of host and user identities in information systems using cryptographic keys, which can later be subjected to verification. The cryptographic methods mean nothing until one has an acceptable level of certainty about identity.

Naming needs to reflect variation in time and space, using version numbers and timestamps, or other virtual locational coordinates. Variation in space can be handled through scope, as it is parallel. However, variation in time is a serial property, indistinguishable from versioning, and therefore naming a set of promises must be unique within a given scope.

Note

A component name or identifier is any representative, promisable attribute, rendered in any medium, that maps uniquely to a set of two promises:

- A description of the promises kept by the component (e.g., text like "Toyota Prius," or a shape like a handle, indicating carrying or opening)

- A description of the model or version in a family or series of evolving designs (e.g., 1984 model, version 2.3, or "panther")

When components evolve through a number of related versions, we often keep a version identifier separate from the functional name because the name anchors the component to a set of broad promises, while the version number promises changes to the details.

Naming in Software Packaging

Computer software is usually separated into *packages*. Naming these packages remains a pernicious problem, because packages do not make clean noncontentious promises.

Packages are commonly named with a main and a version number, for example:

```
flash-player-kde4-11.2.202.243-30.1.x86_64
unzip-6.00-14.1.2.x86_64
myspell-american-20100316-24.1.2.noarch
kwalletmanager-4.7.2-2.1.2.x86_64
```

The main name leads up to a number. Notice that the version numbering needs only to be unique for a given component, as each component essentially lives in its own world branch, designated by the root name.

We cannot promise the uniqueness of names, since we cannot make a promise on behalf of another agent. This creates challenges for addressing entities in computer networks. At best, one can promise to change the name of a component if there is a collision. Thus, naming becomes a contentious issue. Changing the name of a component in a system would have an affect on all parts that referred to it. Conversely, any name that represents a component with identical promises to another component may be considered an alias for the other name.

To avoid this, it is common to limit the scope of name promises voluntarily, into so-called namespaces. Within any particular namespace, the user of the components would normally see value in the uniqueness of names.

Naming Promisee Usage (-) Rather than Function (+)

Every time we make use of a promise, there are two parties: the promiser and the promisee. Sometimes, a functional (+) promise is conditional on input from the agent, who is also the promisee. The input changes the result. The different uses of a reusable promise could be named individually, by the promisee, based on what it feeds to the promiser, for easy distinction. For example, a process agent, consuming input components and their promises, can promise differently named applications, each made from components as if they were separate entities. A collection of transistors, resistors, and capacitors might be a radio or a television. A collection of fabrics might be clothing or a tent. A mathematical function, like a cosine, promises a different result depending on the number fed into it. In each case, the template of the promise is the same, but the details of how it is used vary. This is what we mean by the promise of parameterization.

Parameters are customizing options, and are well understood in computer programming or mathematics. A parameter is something that makes a generic thing unique by plugging a context into the generality.

A description of what input data, parameters, or arguments are being supplied to the component's function supplement the name of the function itself. In computer science, we call this a *function call*. Different function calls promise different outcomes, and, as long as causation is uniquely determined, this is just as good a name as the bundle of promises about what comes out. Indeed, it is probably more convenient, since we know the data we want to feed in, but not necessarily the promised data that comes out.

Attaching distinct names to instances of usage can be useful for identifying when and where a particular component was employed (e.g., when fault finding).

In computer programming, generic components are built into libraries that expose promises to using patterns of information. This is sometimes called an API or Application Programming Interface. The application programmer, or promise user, makes use of the library components in a particular context for a particular purpose. Each usage of a particular component may thus be identified by the information passed to it, or the other components connected to it. We may give each such example a name like "authentication dialogue," "comment dialogue," and so on. We can also use the set of parameters given to an API interface promise as part of the unique name of the reference.

The Cost of Modularity

When does it make economic sense to build components? Each promise carries an expected value, assessed individually by the agents and other components in a system. A promise viewpoint allows us to enumerate costs by attaching the valuations made by each agent individually, from each viewpoint: the eye of the beholder.

Even from the viewpoint of a single agent, the cost associated with a modular design is not necessarily a simple calculation. It includes the ongoing collaborative cost of isolating components into weakly coupled parts, designing their interfaces, and also the cost of maintaining and evolving the parts over time. The accessibility of the parts adds a cost, too. If components are hard to change or maintain because they are inside a closed box, then it might be simpler to replace the whole box. However, if the component is cheap and the rest of the box is expensive in total, then the reckoning is different.

Making tyres into components makes sense. Changing a flat tyre rather than replacing an entire car makes obvious sense, because the tyres are accessible and large, not to mention cheaper than a whole car. Making electronic components like transistors, capacitors, and resistors certainly made sense to begin with, when they were large and experimentation was important. This allowed them to be replaced individually, so it made sense to change failed components individually, thus saving the cost of unnecessary additional replacements. However, the miniaturization of electronics eventually changed this situation.

At some point it became cheap to manufacture integrated circuits that were so small that changing individual components became impractical. Thus the economics of componentization moved towards large-scale integration of parameterizable devices.

Virtual computational components, like software running on virtual servers in a data center, are apparently cheap to replace, and are used extensively to manage the evolution of software services. However, while these components are cheap to build, existing components gather history and contain runtime data that might be expensive to lose.

Modularity is generally considered to be a positive quality in a system, but when does componentization actually hurt?

- When the cost of making and maintaining the components exceeds the cost of just building the total system, over the expected lifetime of the system. (Think of VLSI chips, which are composed of tens of thousands of individual transistors and ancillary components.)

- If the components are not properly adapted to the task because of poor understanding of the patterns of usage. (Think of making do with commodity goods, where custom made would be preferable.)

- If the additional overhead of packaging and connecting the components (combinatorics) exceeds other savings.

- When the number of components becomes so large that it contributes to the cognitive burden of navigating the complexity of the total system. (Think of software that imports dozens of modules into every program file, or a book that assumes too much foreknowledge.)

Some Exercises

1. Think of some examples of business promises. Break these down into the promises made to support these "goals" within the business organization. Now compare this to the organization chart of the business. Do the promises match the job descriptions? Were jobs assigned by wishful thinking, or are they based on what the individual could promise to deliver?

2. Divide and conquer is a well-known concept. Delegating tasks (impositions) to different agents is one way to centrally share the burden of keeping a promise amongst a number of agents. However, it comes with its own cost of coordination.

   Write down a promise you would like to keep, then write down the agencies to which you would like to delegate, and the promises each of them must now make, including the cost of coordinating, without losing coordination. How do you estimate the additional complexity of interacting with multiple agencies, compared to when a single agent was the point of contact? Is this an acceptable cost? When would it (not) be acceptable?

3. Innovation, in technology, can be helped or hindered by componentization. If you split a product into multiple parts, developed with independent responsiblity, the success must be influenced by the degree of coordination of those parts. Think about what this means for the ability to innovate and improve parts independently and together as a whole. Is componentization an illusion, sometimes or always?

4. Very-large–scale integration (VLSI) in computer chips is an example of the opposite of componentization. When does such packing make economic sense? What are the benefits and disadvantages of bundling many promises into a single agency?

5. (For technical readers) Write down the promises that distinguish a process container (e.g., a Docker instance, or a Solaris zone) from a statically compiled binary, running under the same operating system.

7

Service Engineering

It will not come as a surprise that there is a simple connection between the concepts of promises and services. Promises are valuable to other agents when kept reliably, or at last predictably, and they can even be sold or traded. This is the basis of a service.

Service buoys the human experience, on a day-to-day basis. There are dumb services, like web servers and directory service lookups, or ATM cash-point transactions, where we don't expect or even want too much intelligence, but there are also experiential services like hotels and restaurants where humans are directly involved, and the subtle semantics are everything to the assessment of the outcome.

Services make up a potentially complex topic because they are a meeting place between the key ingredients of promises: semantics, dynamics, and valuation.

- Services have to work in detail (semantics).
- Services have to operate at some scale (dynamics).
- Services have to be economically viable to survive (economics).

In this chapter, I want to sketch out a few of these issues. The real power of Promise Theory comes from a more formal, symbolic toolset, but that is the subject of a different book.

Promise Theory makes a simple prediction about services, which is possibly counterintuitive. It tells us that the responsibility for getting service ultimately lies with the client, not the server. That clarifies a few things about the design of systems where services play a role.

The Client-Server Model

The client-server model is one of the classic patterns in information technology, and business. A client is any agent that makes a request, and a server is any agent that responds to the request and performs the service. There are two ways to model this:

- *A client makes a spontaneous imposition upon the server* (i.e., the client "throws a request over the wall," and the server is expected to catch it). This is often the case for an irregular interaction, like buying something from a vending machine, or dropping in for an emergency room visit.
- *A client maintains a continued promise relationship,* with more forethought to arrange mutual promise (e.g., a regular delivery of mail is promised at 10 each morning, and you promise to accept it). A normal doctor's appointment, even though irregular, is usually promised in advance, because doctors do not promise to receive patients without an appointment. The patient is subordinate to the doctor's availability.

If we string together many impositions, it makes sense to negotiate a more formal promise relationship. In other words, the more continuity of intent we have, the more promises rather than impositions make sense.

What promises add is the recognition of an ongoing relationship. An imposition is a *fire and forget* event that exists in the moment it is made, but a promise is something that is known for longer and the time (or times) at which it is kept is not tied to a single moment. Thus, when we think in promises, we plan for more of a relationship of continuous verification. This is what services are all about.

Services Lead to Robust Ecosystems of Intent

Services are important because they are the natural outcome of any scheme of voluntary cooperation. If we disallow the prospect of attacking or coercing others to affect our intent, then the natural expression of intent becomes to *use* what has already been made available.

Every consumer or provider of a service remains the seat of its own power and decision-making, and promising to consume a service that is not yet provided acts as a nonaggressive signal to other agents to voluntarily provide the service, assuming that the economic incentives are mutually beneficial.

Services thus lead naturally to ecosystems of loosely coupled, intentional behaviour, which are documented and measurable through their promises.

Responsibility for Service Delivery

The responsibility for obtaining lies with the client, because no service can be transmitted without the client accepting a service promise from a server. Even if there are multiple servers promising the service redundantly so that the possibility of service is guaranteed, the client needs to make a choice to *use* one or more of them. The client is the single point of failure (see Figure 7-1).

Figure 7-1. A client has to promise to use a service (-) in order to avail itself of the offer (+). No matter how many servers there are, failing or keeping their service promise, the client has to choose and accept a good one. So the client has ultimate responsibility for getting service.

Similarly, if there is no server offering the service and the client needs the service, it is up to the client to locate an agent promising the service and bind to it.

Redundancy, on the provider side, does not immunize against all possible failures; it only increases the likelihood of a user being able to keep a promise to use the service. This should tell us something important. The responsibility for obtaining a service lies with the intent to obtain service (i.e., with the user, not with the provider). A provider can exercise best-effort and no more.

Dispatchers and Queues for Service on Demand

In many services, clients arrive at some kind of queue or waiting area, imposing themselves as clients for service. The existence of the waiting area is effectively a promise to accept their impositions. Clients are assigned a server by an agent called a dispatcher, when one becomes available. For example, customers arrive without an appointment at a restaurant or at an emergency room.

In technology, dispatchers are also called load balancers, as tasks of some magnitude might be shared between multiple servers. For instance, a client might request taxi transport for eight people. A dispatcher might then share the load between two taxis (see Figure 7-2).

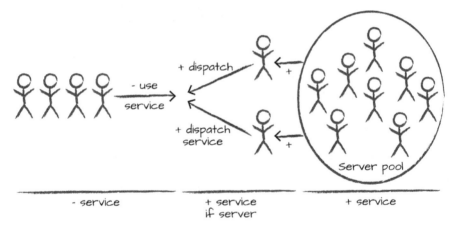

Figure 7-2. A dispatcher can act as a go-between service or proxy for finding a server for incoming clients, but the responsibility to use still lies with the client.

The dispatcher becomes a proxy or broker for the acquisition of a service provider. When many requests arrive, the dispatcher might need to share its load with another dispatcher, too. Quite soon, a hierarchy of service responsibility emerges. However, in all cases, the client has the responsibility of accepting an agent to interact with, so the role of the dispatcher could easily be eliminated if the agent had knowledge of the possible servers.

Delivering Service Through Intermediaries or Proxies

Let's explore the idea of proxies in more depth. Suppose the giver of a promise requires the assistance of other intermediary agents in order to keep its promise. The basic experience of promise conditionals may be used to address this: a server can promise its service conditionally if the proxy promises to assist. Let's examine how such an agent can promise delivery of goods and services through a number of intermediaries. This is the so-called end-to-end delivery problem, and it forms the basis of many similar patterns, including postal delivery agents, transportation agents, publishers, cabling infrastructure, waiters, actors, postal workers, contractors, and even buses.

Schematically, we typically imagine the problem as a story-line narrative, as in Figure 7-3.

Figure 7-3. Schematic service delivery through a proxy or intermediate agent.

This figure is a simplistic after-the-fact idealization of what actually happens during a single enactment of events to keep a promise once. It does not represent a state of process continuity. What happens if the item or service is not delivered? How does this distinguish discrete packages (like books) from continuous streams (like video)? Table 7-1 provides some examples of proxy delivery.

Table 7-1. Examples of proxy delivery

Server	Proxy	Client
Factory	Truck	Showroom
Player	Ball	Player
Music	Stereo system	Listener
Phone company	Phone	Phone client

Framing Promises as State or Action

Although I've deliberately focused on a singular view of promises, there are two ways we could formulate even a chain of promises: as an imperative sequence of relative changes, or as a declarative statement of a desired end state. In general, the latter is preferred for its robustness and consistency.

Consider the different formulations:

- Promise to act (push delivery, make a relative change)
- Promise the final outcome (continuous pull, assure outcome)

The first of these represents a discrete, one-time delivery of the outcome to the agent, which might be satisfied but is never repeated. Indeed, it cannot be, because it promises something relative to a state that also promises to destroy that state. There is also the possibility that the state changes before the promise can be kept, so the value of the imperative promise is somewhat in doubt.

For example, a slalom skier could make a series of promises to use the ski markers, or could simply promise to get to the bottom, without observing such constraints (Figure 7-4). These two are related by conditions. The push promises:

1. I promise to go to post 1, then

2. I promise to go to post 2.

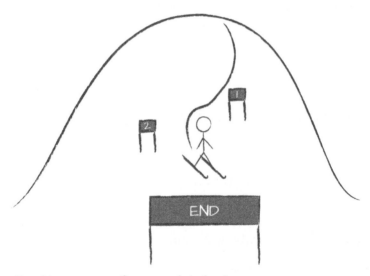

Figure 7-4. Promising a sequence of steps, or a desired end state.

The conditional end state promises:

1. I promise to be at post 1, and then this promise expires.

2. I promise to be at post 2 if I have been at post 1.

Once the promise of a single event has been kept, it is usually kept just once. To repeat a promised event, or make a replacement, we would require a new and different promise altogether. Thus we can write promises in the first form, where they can also behave like prearranged impositions. This is called an imperative pattern. Alternatively we can write them in the second form, representing a continuous attempt to ensure that the agent always achieves the outcome. This is called a declarative or desired end-state pattern.

This second kind of statement can persist for an indefinite time, and the state of the agent can be maintained, even for future slalom races. Thus it documents more than a single event in time. This is important, because, in the world of services, time is not a very interesting variable. Services are usually delivered as steady-state processes (i.e., so-called continuous delivery).

Although we envisage agents in a continual state of readiness to keep promises, impositions may be quenched only once, since the states they depend on are lost in a timeline. Continuous promises kept on-demand last for extended times. We may use these extreme positions to model multiagent workflows that are either one-off triggered events or continuous flows.

APIs and Policy Systems in IT

IT systems are steered by one of two user experiences that could be roughly divided into Application Programming Interfaces (APIs) and Policy-Based Management (PBM). APIs represent an imposition model of service, while PBM represents a declaration of fixed promises.

With an API, service (-) promises, made by promised commands, are triggered by impositions that follow an overarching script for "orchestrated" change. The desired outcome is "getting through the script," but the end state is not defined absolutely. There are promises here, but they are only tiny parts of a longer, undefined narrative. The promise of an API is to subordinate control to the consumer of its services. The API agents essentially promise to relinquish their autonomy and be steered by the user.

In a PBM, the outcomes of promises need only parameterization, and, once completed, represent complete end states. No larger narrative is needed to bring a system into a stable target state. Parameterization of the fixed promises is generally supplied by some kind of declarative language. The promise of PBM is to reduce the uncertainty inherent in an incomplete narrative by fixing promises in advance, except for some configuration data.

There is much debate over which approach is best, but PBM systems have been growing in popularity since the early 1990s. The price of the API model is that each new imposition requires new communication, leading to poor scaling. Policy-based systems are common in highly scalable architectures, where autonomous agents save communication overheads by retaining their independence.

Delivery Chains by Imposition

The delivery chain is an important abstraction that applies across a whole range of different industries. A lot of different service-oriented workflows can be cast in this image. As the length of the chain gets longer, the complexity of trust relationships becomes very complex, so I'll restrict this discussion to a single intermediary agent or proxy, as shown in Figure 7-5. As usual, there are two approaches to delivery.

For blind trust, a widely used pattern for working is the "fire and forget" imposition pattern.[5]

---

5 This is not without its problems, and has been much criticized in recent years. In IT development and deployment, this led to the DevOps movement.

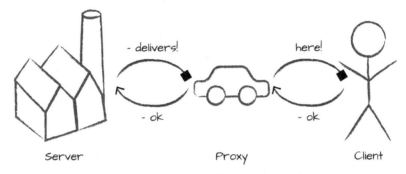

Figure 7-5. Imposition-based workflow, or "fire and forget."

Fire and forget is an event-driven view; the server tries to push a change or delivery by imposing it on the delivery agent. This is called *fire and forget* because the trigger event does not seek or obtain any assurance of final outcome. The intermediary or proxy promises to accept such impositions.

- Server imposes "take this delivery" onto Proxy (-D1)
- Proxy promises "accept delivery" to Server (-D1)
- Proxy imposes "take this delivery" to Client (-D2)
- Client promises "accept delivery" to Proxy (-D2)

We need a more mathematical notation to make these promises precise, but the basic intent should be clear from Figure 7-5.

This approach is based on ephemeral impositions, without any assessment. These are clearly fragile. What if the imposition is not accepted, or was dropped accidentally? If the chain fails somewhere, it would require a new imposition to restart the intended sequence of events. In the absence of a promise to achieve a desired outcome, there is no implication that the agents would try more than once to keep the promise. As a result, the server ends up with no assurances about what happens at the client end.

Delivery Chains with Promises

What if we use promises and desired end states instead of impositions? This implies a more long-standing relationship between the parties. Take a look at Figure 7-6.

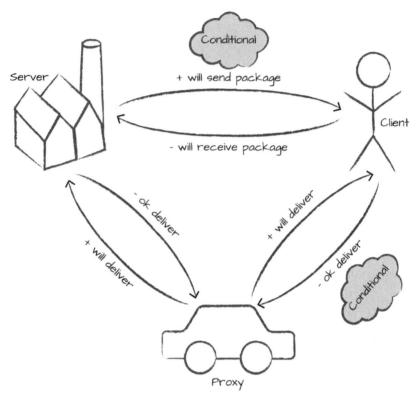

Figure 7-6. Desired state, self-maintaining workflow, or assured delivery. Documenting all conditionals in promises is a more honest way of bookkeeping fragile dependencies.

The server promises the client end state, such as the delivery of some good or service: "You will have the package," conditional on "if the delivery agent promises delivery." The server also promises to use a promise to deliver the package from the proxy: "Deliver package to client." Recall that the combination of these two promises may be written more simply, by the law of conditional assistance, as:

- Server promises to "provide service if proxy promises delivery" to client
- Server uses a "promise to deliver to client" from proxy

By the law of conditional promising, this may be considered a promise, albeit a conditional one, because the client has sufficient information that the server is covering its requirements:

- Server promises "delivery conditionally on proxy" to client

We can now use this last item as a shorthand for the two preceding promises.

This all sounds like a simple thing, but it leads to a surprising amount of complexity in terms of promises. Remember that these promises have to follow the rules of binding and only promising an agent's own behaviour. When we follow through this discipline, we end up with a plainly accurate version of documented cooperation, but at a level of detail that we might not have been expecting.

The full collaboration now takes the form:

- Server promises "delivery conditionally if proxy delivers" (P if D) to client (+)
- Server promises "to provide package" (+P) AND "to use delivery service" (-D) to proxy
- Proxy promises "to deliver packages" (+D) AND to "accept packages" (-P) server
- Proxy promises "package conditionally if server provides" (D if P) client (+)
- Client promises to accept the terms "delivery conditionally if proxy delivers" (P if D) server (-)
- Client promises to accept the terms "package conditionally if server provides" (D if P) proxy (-)

The bindings are now complete. We have a total of eight (shortened) promises for this simple exchange between three parties. It might be a surprise just how many promises we need to have explicit documentation or assurance of the behaviours of the agents. This is one of the aspects of thinking in promises that is most valuable. By following a straightforward, logical discipline, the complexity of cooperation unravels before our eyes, revealing all of the things that might go wrong.

Reliable and Unreliable Services as Proxy Virtualization

In IT, there is the concept of *reliable* and *unreliable* services. These terms are used especially in connection with data communications, and are represented by the two Internet transport layer services TCP and UDP, which are operated via the proxy IP and MAC layers (the so-called Layers 2 and 3 of the OSI network model, respectively).

An unreliable service (like UDP) is an impositional "fire and forget" approach to communication. It assumes that some promiser is listening for signals, and packets are then imposed on the receiver at random.

A reliable service (like TCP) establishes a *handshake* or promise binding, in which both sides promise to acknowledge delivery of information, or try again until they are satisfied that the promises have been kept. Reliable protocols have an overhead.

Both services run on top of IP and MAC, which act as delivery proxies for the end-to-end promises to be kept. The proxy thus presents itself as a virtual path or connection between the client and the server. The IP and MAC services themselves rely on hardware proxies. If one dissected the whole tower of promises required to document this system of reliances explicitly, it would be mind-bogglingly complex. This is why unreliable services are used for nearly all the steps and proxies along the way, and the overarching reliability is left to a high-level virtual promise like a TCP connection. The assumption here is that the underlying layers can always be trusted to give best-effort, and that any failure is a glitch that will be repaired by trying again.

Formality Helps the Medicine Go Down

As the length of cooperative chains increases beyond a single proxy or intermediary, it is difficult to represent all of these promise interactions without a more formal language. The full version of Promise Theory requires a mathematical formulation, but for now it suffices to add the labels (P,D) in the manifest, and we see how the circuitry of + and - promises connects.

The symmetries between + and - polarities in the promise collaboration, and between P and D, indicate the complementarity of the promises. The server promises its client, "I will give you P if the delivery agent promises you D." The delivery agent says, "I will deliver D if I receive P from the server." Both agencies are promising the client something that requires them to work together, and the only difference between them from the client's viewpoint is the realization of how the promises are kept.

This promise from the server to the client represents a virtual interface between the two, which could not be represented at all in the push-imposition model. It represents the effective promise from the server to the client, and the client accepts.

1. In two promises, the server promises to deliver the end state "package received" (P) via the proxy delivery agent.

2. To accomplish this, the server promises to hand over the package (+P) to the proxy, and the proxy promises to accept such transactions (-P).

3. The proxy promises the server that it can deliver (+D) to the client.

4. The delivery agent promises to deliver what it received from the server (+D if P), because it needs confirmation (-D if P) from the client that it is OK to deliver, assuming that condition P was quenched by P being kept. Equivalently, it will deliver when the client makes its pull request to acquire the delivery.

This might all seem like a lot of fuss. Importantly, it reveals the intricacies we take for granted in making promises through an intermediary.

The neat thing about Promise Theory is that it turns these complicated considerations into a simple, symbolic algebra. If you are not mathematically inclined, think of it as a simple bookkeeping methodology.

Chains of Intermediaries

Suppose there is not just one intermediary, but a chain, like a game of Chinese whispers. This happens by recursion. The delivery agent (a contractor for the server) subcontracts the delivery to another company. Then we have to repeat the proxy relationship between the first proxy and the second proxy. But additionally, now the first proxy promise has to be conditional on the second, so the original server is informed of this subcontracting through the change of promise. Similarly, the additional promises to assure that the first proxy will indeed engage the second, the third, and so on, must be added. The client also needs to have a relationship with the subcontractor.

The details quickly become complex without a more formal language to represent the promises. If you want to see the formal solution, take a look at the mathematical treatment of Promise Theory.[5] The result is quite beautiful in its symmetry properties.

It might seem surprising just how many promises need to be documented to accomplish something we do all the time. What is the difference between this and a chain of relative pushes? There, each agent merely throws a task "over the wall" to the next agent (this is sometimes called *fire and forget*).

If we use promises, our expectations are higher, but our blind trust that the outcome will come to pass is lower. We seek the assurance of a promise. This example represents the extreme end of obtaining maximum certainty through signalling of intent. For continuous delivery scenarios, this represents the minimum level of assurance for a process to be fully managed.

Trust is cheap, and verification is expensive. The cost of fully promised continuous end-to-end delivery grows as the order of the number of intermediary agents squared. This cost of an end-to-end assurance can be compared to the cost for the *fire and forget* approach, with only nearest neighbour assurances, which is linear to the number of agents. We thus see the up-front appeal of leaving things to chance.

End-to-End Integrity

In the worst case, one might make no promises between agents and simply see what happens. The usefulness of documenting and making all of these promises lies in seeing how information about agents' intentions needs to flow, and where potential points of failure might occur due to a lack of responsiveness in keeping the promises.

A chain of trust is implicit in any collaboration, with or without promises. Without every agent talking to their dependencies and dependers, a service agent would not be able to detect if any intermediate proxy were to distort one of the promises. Thus the lack of trust in the proxies drives us to require more promises conditionally. This adds further overhead and expense.

In many real-world situations, one opts to trust agents without explicit promises, simply because this cost of tracking and verifying becomes too much to understand and follow up on.

---

5 See *Promise Theory: Principles and Applications.*

In daily life, such promises are often made in a punitive form through legal contracts, under a threat of retribution for failure to comply with terms in a contract. This also turns out to be costly, as lawyers perform this exercise in a language of verbal warfare rather than cooperation.

Transformation Chains or Assembly Lines

The final generalization of the previous section is where agents do not merely pass along a service while maintaining its integrity; each agent also makes a change in the manner of an assembly line. This pattern is common in factories and product packaging companies.

A typical application for this kind of model is the scenario depicted in Figure 7-7, in which a product is designed and then built and distributed to customers through a delivery chain. Although we want to think in terms of this narrative, the reality of ensuring cooperation throughout the process is much more complicated. The same promise model sheds light on this case, too.

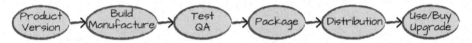

Figure 7-7. Schematic production line for goods or services.

Again, it is this issue of trust (or conversely the need for verification of intermediate steps) that leads to complexity in the promise graph. As more verification is expected, we approach a full set of promises between all of the agents, with every agent telling every other agent of its intent.

As intermediate agents promise more radical or sensitive transformations of data, trust in their promises by the point of service could become harder to swallow. Thus one can easily imagine that the most efficient delivery chains are those that make simple, harmless, and unambiguous promises.

Continuity of Delivery and Intent

When a system promises continuous operation, none of the promises may become invalid or be removed from the picture as a result of a failure to keep any promise (i.e., promises are described for all times and conditions, in a continuous, steady state).

Continuous delivery is what you get when you fly in a plane. The plane should not drop out of the sky while the service is being provided. As well as continuity of execution, there is continuity of purpose. When you fly in a plane, the plane should fly to a single destination and not be changing its mind all the time. Promises have to last as long as it takes to keep them, else they become deceptions. What makes a promise view valuable is that it allows us to define and document the virtual interface between client and server—or customer and provider —and to abstract away the helper agent. So what happens when we want to make a change?

Automation has become an important strategy for policing continuity of intent. Machines are excellent at validating rigid behaviours, without having to burden a human with a tight relationship with service specifics. We humans have a small and finite number of Dunbar slots to wield for our attention spans, and we want to spend them wisely. Machines can engage with mechanisms and humans can engage with humans (see Figure 7-8).

Figure 7-8. The promise of automation is to free up repetitive relationships whose only purpose is to assess inhuman promises.

In quality assurance schemes, product acceptance tests are used to create surrogate relationships that engage with a service to check whether it is keeping its promises.[5] Such tests don't promise quality, as such, rather they are trip wires that promise to detect unintended breakage of promises.

---

5 CFEngine is an information technology automation tool that uses the concept of promises to embed testing of every promise at a fundamental level.

The Versioning Problem Again

As service providers learn and adapt to new situations, they naturally want to change the promises they make. This presents a conundrum for clients who are not ready to accept change. Service transfer requires there to be a matching binding between the give and take. In the worst case, promise bindings might be broken as a service agent fails to keep a promise on which a client relies. To deal with this issue, we use the concept of versions to keep parallel "worlds" alive without conflict.

A set of promises represents a product or service offering, and we want to be able to evolve that set of promises.

For uninterrupted, consistent experience, a user of promises expects:

- Continuity of delivery (dynamics)

- Continuity of intent (semantics)

But for long-term satisfaction, clients also want:

- Continuity of improvement (changing semantics)

Many service users pay for improvements as part of the service. This is especially true in the software industry, where bug fixes are common, and it is actually possible to use a new version of a product after as little as a few minutes.

Avoiding Conflicting Promises by Branching into Separate Worlds

To avoid breaking existing products and services, the industry has learned to use version branching, so that we can pursue the illusion of being able to make many changes in one version without conflicting with another version. This is a kind of namespace.

Promising essential continuity of operation during a change is perfectly possible with a promise view of the world because each version becomes an independent agent, with its own namespace. In information technology, *virtual machines* and *application containers* represent such namespaces.

Recall that we define agents as parts of a system that can change independently. At any time, a collection of promises could be duplicated, like cells dividing, and then altered. This is the mechanism used in information technology for forking runtime processes, and also in the forking of development projects in version control (for example, git).

Users can choose which bundle of promises to accept and hence bind to, as long as multiple versions are kept alive (see Figure 7-9). Clearly, we can repeat this branching process as many times as we like. But the cost of keeping all the promises grows exponentially.

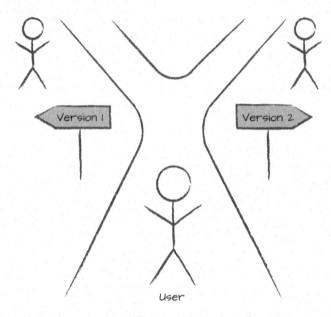

Figure 7-9. Branching of promises into different worlds avoids conflict. Different versions become separate autonomous agents, making different bundles of promises.

Avoiding Many Worlds' Branches by Converging on Target

The faster we want to make changes to a service, the more versions we end up branching off. This could quickly become a problem. In product development, there is the concept of continuous delivery. This is about promising the semantic consistency and availability of every version of an evolving product design, as quickly as the changes are made.

If new branches were made for every small change, it would quickly pass beyond the ability of users to keep track of them, so an alternative strategy is needed. Instead of making evolving versions always coexist, to avoid conflicting promises, we can also make sure that changes preserve the same promises throughout versions by collapsing the multiple worlds back into fewer worlds (see Figure 7-10). In other words, we counteract divergence with convergence.

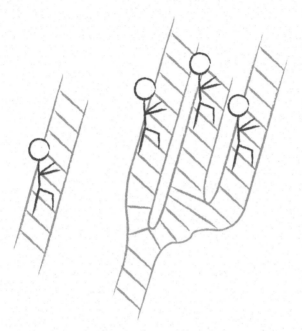

Figure 7-10. Climbing the version ladder, aka the stairway to heaven. To counteract the ladders, we can create snakes/chutes that collapse the branches back into fewer worlds.

Given a new intended outcome, we know that we can converge to a reliable product, without waste or conflict, as long as there are only weak dependencies between the components. Thus we never change any promised intentions. The only changes we should make would be to fix promise implementations, leading to promises that were made but not kept in earlier versions.

The idea of continuous delivery in product and service development is thus to de-emphasize thinking about major version releases that have to branch to co-exist, in favour of a continuum of incremental improvements that converge to a stable end state through an ongoing process.

Not all continuous delivery pipelines are about software development. The airline industry, for example, does a pretty good job of delivering continuous back-to-back flights by scheduling infrastructure slots. Schedules and flight plans change slowly, but adjustments may be made on the fly to adapt continuously to conditions.

Backwards Compatibility Means Continuity of Intent

So what we're saying is simply that, if new versions break compatibility, then they break promises to users, and prevent users from accepting the new promises. If changes are made without knowing what the promises are supposed to be, there is no way to gauge whether they were successful or not because there is no record of intent.

Writing specifications is not the same as making a promise. A specification is only part of a recipe to change or build something; it still doesn't document what the thing is for. So, if promises are not explicit, a service user has to go through a lengthy process of assessing changes to decide whether the new version is compatible with older versions, or simply whether it is useful.

Assessing a Service by Promising to Use It (Testing)

Assessing these service promises is the job of product testing. The likelihood of keeping promises is not improved by testing for correct outcomes, but by determining the correct intended outcomes in the first place. In other words, service quality comes from formulating promises, not from checking that they were kept. Nevertheless, testing is useful as a trip wire for unintended change.

Making promises up front separates intent from implementation for products and services. It separates design from execution and implementation. Version branching (divergence) is a tool to avoid conflicts of interest by keeping separate intentions apart. Continuous integration (convergence) is a tool used for avoiding conflicts by maintaining constancy of purpose. The former gives more freedom, but the latter is exponentially cheaper.

These techniques are widely used in software development today, and there seems to be some confusion about why versioning is important. The purpose of versioning is not to be able to undo missteps and allow developers to take less care in what they do. Intent is not transactional, but implementation might be. The idea of rolling back implementations is a piece of transaction processing mimicry. If we treat changes as transactions, then we make changes without intent. If we make a mistake in service delivery, we should correct the forward semantic process (i.e., the design), and the dynamical follow-up will maintain the target outcome.

A typical goal is therefore that newer versions would be compatible, drop-in substitutes for old versions. How do we know the design itself will converge to have the same fitness for purpose, with forward and backward compatibility? One way is to avoid too much branching and to correct continuously without change of intent. It is just basic maintenance, fixing promises that were not kept. As long as error correction is so fast that consumers can't really see it happening, they will not be able to assess whether promises were not kept.

Componentization can help here (Figure 7-11). Modularity, or putting semantics into fixed buckets, helps convergence to a predictable set of end states.[5] If your product is really a bundle of independent promises, then every promise can converge independently of every other, without interference or waiting. Even the order doesn't matter, and parallel factories could be used to keep the component promises, to build the parts to be assembled later.

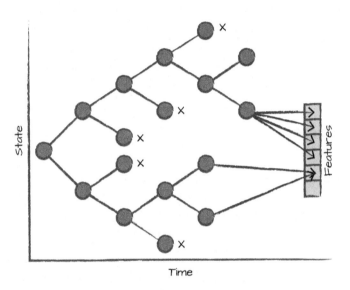

Figure 7-11. As we climb the version ladder, branching can be counteracted by ensuring that all the branches map into the same set of desired outcomes, or semantic buckets.

When every change version is backwards compatible (maintaining the set of compatible promises), you are converging, not breaking, earlier versions; and all changes reach a desired asymptotic end state, whether you are explicitly modular or not. It is a convergence of convergences, a semantic waterfall. Many worlds collapse back into one. Backwards compatibility is ensured when promises

---

5 Here, computer programmers might think of hash tables or Bloom filters as tools for this kind of semantically stable vector of outcomes.

converge to a fixed, desired state and are kept continuously, even as the scope and details of the promises grow.

Services Are Intended to Reduce Complexity for Clients

The purpose of a service abstraction is to fix the semantics of an interaction between a client and a provider, so that a clear outcome will result from a simple request. Fixing and reducing the parameters to a minimum reduces the information needed to achieve the desired end state, and reduces the number of conditional dependencies that might lead to promises not being kept. The value of a service lies in its simplicity (i.e., the extent to which it can reduce an expensive interaction to a simpler one). To be trusted by potential clients, services have to advertise their promises clearly, including risks.

Some Exercises

1. Imagine an online service, like a hotel reservation. Is the hotel run as a policy-based system, or as an API user interface? What are the promises made by the hotel? What is the API or policy declaration language? What proxies does the hotel service use to perform its services?

2. Imagine a system of ordering a parking space in a parking lot by pre-arranged promise instead of by imposition. What would that look like? What does this analogy tell you about IT systems?

3. Discuss to what extent a book can be viewed as a service. What role does the book play? What proxies are involved in the service (hint: is this an ebook, or do you wear glasses?)

4. Think of an online music or video streaming service. What promises are made by the provider? What happens if the service becomes unavailable, is there a backup? What proxies are involved in the delivery of the streaming service?

8

Knowledge and Information

There is a saying that if you have one clock you know what time it is, but if you have two you are not sure. The joke is about a fundamental issue with autonomous agencies. When everyone lives in a private world, how would they come to agree about anything—in fact, would they ever need to? Whom should we trust? Who has the right answer? Do facts have any meaning? What can we say, at all, about who knows what about whom, and where?

Relativity leads to all manner of trouble and intrigue in the world of agents, human or otherwise. This is certainly one of the issues that Promise Theory attempts to get to the bottom of by decomposing the world into autonomous pieces, and then documenting their probable behaviours, even in the face of incomplete information.

How Information Becomes Knowledge

As we've already discussed, knowledge is a body of information that's familiar (i.e., that you know like a friend). We sample information from the world through observation, hopefully adding the context in which the observations were made, until we've rehearsed that relationship. Our level of confidence about what we see only grows through this repetition. That's why experimentalists repeat experiments many times, and why data samples need to be repeated. It is about whether we promise to accept information as fact or reject it as conjecture. This status emerges over time as we repeatedly revisit the same measurements and ask the same questions.

Knowledge: The Mystery Cat

We seek it here, we seek it there. The agency of knowledge is nowhere and everywhere! Agents can promise to give and accept information, but we cannot tell whether that information will be absorbed and understood by every agent in the same way. So how do we arrange for agents within some system or organization to become knowledgeable according to a measurable or approved standard?

Knowledge must be individual because it is based on promises to accept information (-). Knowledge is accepted in the eye of the beholder, by each individual agent. That means that each agent has its knowledge as a private world or branch of reality. If an agent wants to claim knowledge of something, it must promise (+): "I promise that fact X means (insert explanation) to me."

Suppose then that someone asks the agent the question: "Is fact X known to be true?" The agent can answer for itself. If the question were asked open-endedly to many agents, we would really be asking: "Is there a consensus among you agents; i.e., is there some regularity to the promises all you agents make about X?"

For example, two clocks are two agents. Do they make the same promise about the time? Two humans are two agents. Do they both promise to know the name of the President of the United States? Do they agree? If they agree, do they agree by accident, or by cooperation?

If we want to engineer the knowledge of agents, to try to induce a consensus, we need to solicit the acceptance of all parts of the system. This is just as much of a problem in technology, where data has to be distributed over many computers, as it is for humans.

Passing Information Around

Let's put it another way. We could call a sample of data a passerby. Then information might be called an acquaintance, and knowledge a real friend. If we want to promise to turn data into knowledge, a chance encounter into friendship, we need to engage with it, promise to accept it, assimilate it, and revisit it regularly.

As we know from Dunbar, the number of relationships we can really know is limited by our need for detail. If we can reduce the detail to a minimum, we have a strategy for coping. Labelling things in categories, to reduce the number of knowledge relationships, is how we do this. Here, I'm talking, of course, about human categories, not the mathematical variety of category theory, which makes up an altogether different kind of cat. Generalization is a simple example of identifying a promise role amongst a number of agencies of knowledge (facts, exemplars, and relationships).

If I say that I am an expert on subject X, it is a kind of promise that I know a lot about what happens inside the category of X.

Once we are comfortable in our own trusted knowledge, passing it on to others is a whole new story, in which the recipient is always the one calling the shots. Others don't choose our friends for us. You cannot make a promise on behalf of anyone else.

Agents can't promise trust on behalf of one another, so each agent needs to form its own trusted relationship with data to perform the alchemy of turning data into knowledge.

Transmitted information becomes knowledge when it is known (i.e., when it is familiar enough to be trusted and contextualized). Agents experience the world from the viewpoint of the information available to them. Each can form its own independent conclusions and categorize it with its own roles.

Categories Are Roles Made into Many World Branches

We discussed branching in connection with the coexistence of versions, where different promises could live in different agent worlds to avoid conflicting. In the same way, knowledge can avoid having conflicting meanings and interpretations by placing it into different agents. As usual, there is a (+) way and a (-) way:

- The (-) is what we've already discussed. The eye of the individual agent immediately places knowledge in its own world.

- An agent promising its own knowledge (+) can also separate concepts into different branches within itself. This is called a taxonomy or ontology. These branches are called categories or classes.

Categories are an attempt to use the many-worlds branching concept to hide information (Figure 8-1). We can understand this easily by appealing to the idea of roles. A collection of agents or things that is assessed by a user as making the same kind of promise (or collection of promises) forms a role. A role can thus label a category.

Figure 8-1. Cat(egorie)s are in the eye of the beholder. Cat(ch) them if you can!

Patterns like this tie in with the use of repetition to emphasize learning, as mentioned before, and thus patterns are related to our notion of learning by rote. They don't really exist, except in the eye of the beholder: "You may seek him in the basement, you may look up in the air, but I tell you once and once again the category's not there!" (apologies to T.S. Eliot).

A knowledge category is a label that applies to individual bits of knowledge. Each agency might promise a role by association. We can define such roles simply in terms of the promises they make:

- The knowledge itself brands itself with some category label (+).

- Or the user of information files it under some category of their own (-).

- Or knowledge items self-organize into a collaborative role.

Superagent Aggregation (Expialidocious)

Bringing a number of concepts (or agencies of knowledge) together under a common umbrella is what we mean by categorization. We see this as an important part of knowledge management, and it's not hard to see why. It is much cheaper to form a relationship with a container that doesn't reveal more than its name. If we had to have a deep relationship with every internal organ in our friends and relatives, it would quite likely change our perception of them!

A superagent is just a collection of agents that form a collaborative role because of underlying promises to work together. In the extreme case of knowing nothing of what happens to the individual components inside, it is like a black box.

The attachment of a concept such as radio to a set of collaborating relationships is nothing like the naming that happens in a standard taxonomy: it is an interpretation, based on a likely incomplete understanding of the structure of the internal properties, based on an evaluation of its behaviour. In a hierarchical decomposition, one would separate the components into rigid categories like "resistor," capacitor," "transistor," or "plastic" and "metal," none of which say anything about what these parts contribute to.

A radio is thus a collection of subagents with an emergent property (i.e., a collaborative network of properties whose collective promise has no place in a taxonomic categorization related to its parts). The function "radio" is a cooperative role. Emergence is the opposite of categorization.

There might be different categories of radio, of course, at this higher level, such as a two-way radio (walkie-talkie), or a broken radio, which fails to keep its emergent promise. A user would only guess the latter if the radio had packaging that signalled the promise.

A radio is not really more than the sum of its parts, as we sometimes like to say, but its function seems to be, as it forms a collaboration that comes alive and takes on a new interpretation at a different level. Cooperation simply and unmysteriously allows new promises to be made at each cooperative scale. These are not to be found within any single component: they are irreducible, and hence the promises of the whole may be accounted for as a simple sum of the cooperative promises, together with the component promises.

Typical taxonomic decompositions are reductionistic, leaving no room for the understanding of this as a collective phenomenon. This defect can really only be repaired if we understand that it is the *observer* or recipient, not the designer, that ultimately makes the decision whether to accept that the assessment of a set of component promises is a radio or not.

The concept of a radio is clearly much cheaper to maintain as a new and separate entity than as a detailed understanding of how the components collaborate to produce the effect. We frequently use this kind of information hiding to reduce the cost of knowledge, but it is clear that knowledge gets lost in this process. Black boxes allow us to purposefully forget or discard knowledge in order to reduce the cost of accepting a collective role.

The ability to replace a lot of complexity with a simple label brings great economic efficiency for end users of knowledge, which one could measure in concepts per role. It is not the size of a group or role that is the best indicator for providing a reduction in perceived complexity, but rather the affinity that a receiver who promises to use this role's defining pattern feels for the concept. In other words, how well does a user identify or feel resonance with the pattern?

The important point here, as we see repeatedly, is that it is how these terms are perceived by the user (i.e., the *usage*, not the definition) of these terms that is the crucial element here. What is offered is only a prerequisite. It is what is accepted by agents that is important.

Thinking in Straight Lines

Promises come from autonomous, standalone agents. Facts and events are such agents. But humans don't think in terms of standalone facts; we are creatures of association. We love to string together facts into story lines, especially when we communicate in speech or writing. Conditional promises allow us to do this in the framework of promise theory, too.

The concept of a story or narrative is large in human culture, but as far as I can tell, very little attention has been given to its importance to the way we think and reason. A table of contents in a book promises a rough outline of the story told by the book at a very high level. It promises a different perspective on a book's content than the index does (which is designed for random access). A story is thus a collection of topics connected together by associations in a causative thread.

Causality (i.e., starting point "cause" followed by subsequent "effect") promises associative relationships such as "affects" or "always happens before," "is a part of," and so on. These relationships have a transitivity that most promised associations do not have, and this property allows a kind of automated reasoning that is not possible with arbitrary associations.

Understanding more about the principles of automated story or narrative identification as sequences of promises could also have more far-reaching consequences for knowledge than just automated reasoning. In school, not all students find it easy to make their own stories from bare facts, and this could be why some students do better than others in their understanding. We tend to feel we understand something when we can tell a convincing story about it. With more formal principles behind an effort to understand stories, technology could help struggling students grasp connections better, and one could imagine a training program to help basic literacy skills.

Knowledge Engineering

Knowledge engineering includes teaching, storytelling, indoctrination, and even propaganda. From a promise perspective, it has to be based on autonomous cooperation. In the past, this has been done by imposition. Standard stories, official taxonomies of species, or subject categories have been imposed on us from Victorian times. In today's Internet culture, this is all changing.

In the pre-Internet world, we used directory services to navigate information with which we were only loosely acquainted. Directory services, such as tables of contents, tried to organize information within categorized branches such as chapters and sections. This is a good way of arranging a narrative structure when we need to parse information from start to finish. But once search engines, which work like indices, became common, the usefulness of directories and tables of contents was greatly reduced.

The reason is very easy to understand. A directory promises information, as long as you promise to know where to look for it. The cost of being able to find information in the right category is not trivial. The user of a taxonomy or ontology, or list of chapters, has to know a fair amount about that model before it can be used in a helpful way. An index, while offering less narrative context, requires no foreknowledge of a commonly agreed model, and it can offer all of the possible interpretations to scan through. Search engines have made this experience very consumable, and they allow agencies of knowledge to stand alone without narrative constraints, so that users can assess their own narratives as they use the data.

By stripping away unnecessary structure, a promise approach to knowledge grants knowledge the freedom to evolve in a direction dictated by common, collaborative culture.

The Victorian vision of divide-and-conquer taxonomy was naive. The likelihood that we would ever classify meaning into a single, standard, crystalline tree of life is about the same as the likelihood of unifying all the world's cultures into one. The cultural evidence suggests that human social interaction evens out our ideas about categories through mixing and creating "norms." Concepts swarm through the crowd, and we adjust them to follow the influences of others, out of a promise to cooperate. This brings about a condensation from noise to clarity.

The eye of the beholder is fickle and evolving. The final answers about knowledge management probably lie with social anthropology. It will be a challenge for more empirical studies to come up with evidence for the success or failure of the suggestions contained here. In the meantime, there seems to be little to lose by trying a promise approach, so I leave it to the reader to explore these simple guidelines in practice.

Equilibrium and Common Knowledge

Let's return to the bread and butter of moving information around a collection of autonomous agents to achieve a common view. When all agents have consistent knowledge they reach an equilibrium of exchanging values and agreeing with one another. To say that they know says more than that they have accepted the information; it is a more significant promise.

There are two extremes for doing this (see Figure 8-2). The simplest way to achieve common knowledge is to have all agents assimilate the knowledge directly from a single (centralized) source agent. This minimizes the potential uncertainties, and the source itself can be the judge of whether the appropriate promises have been given by all agents mediating in the interaction. The single source becomes an appointed role. This is the common understanding of how a directory or lookup service works.

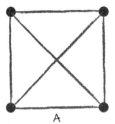 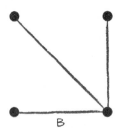

Figure 8-2. Two routes to equilibration again, for knowledge promises.

Although simplest, the centralized source model is not better than one in which data is passed on epidemically from peer to peer. Agents may still have consistent knowledge from an authoritative source, either with or without centralization of communication, but it takes time for agents to settle on their final answer for the common view.

If two agents promise to share one another's knowledge and can both verify that they agree based on some criteria, then it is fair to say that they have consistent knowledge. We should note that, because promises include semantics, and assessment is an integral part of this, consistency requires them to interpret the mutual information in a compatible way, too.

We can express this with the following promises. Suppose agent A knows fact *a*, and agent B knows fact *b*; to say that *a* and *b* are consistent requires what's shown in Figure 8-3.

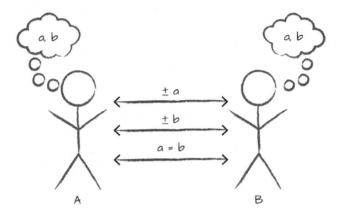

Figure 8-3. Passing on a value received on trust.

A bit more precisely, we can say it like this:

- A promises the information *a* to B (+).

- B promises to accept the information *a* from A (-).

- B promises the information *b* to A.

- A promises to accept the information *b* from B.

- A promises that *a = b* to B.

- B promises that *b = a* to A.

Consistency of knowledge is a strong concept. An agent does not *know* the data unless it is either the source of the knowledge, or it has promised to accept and assimilate the knowledge from the source.

Integrity of Information Through Intermediaries

Knowledge can be passed on from agent to agent with integrity, but we've all seen the game of Chinese whispers. Because information received is in the eye of the beholder, agents can very easily end up with a different picture of the information as a result of their local capabilities and policies for receiving and relaying information.

Take a look at the following three scenarios for passing on information.

1. Accepted from a source, ignored, and passed on to a third party intact, but with no assurance (see Figure 8-4).

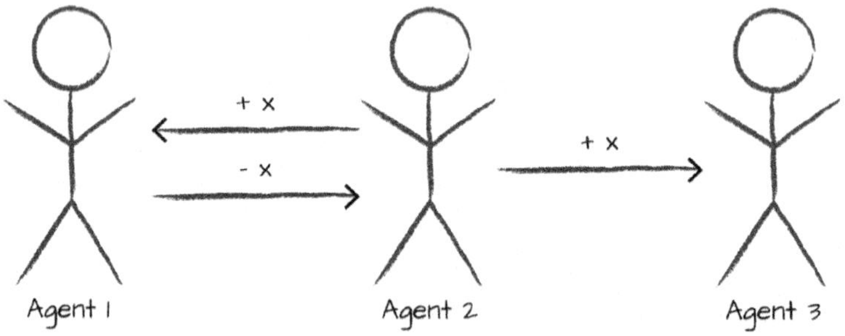

Figure 8-4. Passing on a value received on trust.

Note that agent 2 does not assimilate the knowledge here by making its own version equal to the one it accepted; it merely passes on the value as hearsay.

2. Accepted from a source, ignored, and local knowledge is then passed on to a third party instead. Here agent 1 accepts the information, but instead of passing it on, passes on its own version. The source does not know that agent 2 has not relayed its data with integrity (see Figure 8-5).

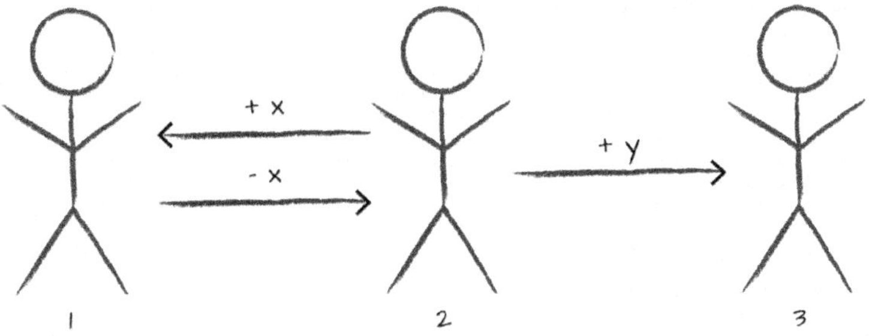

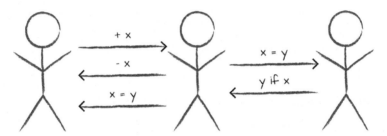

Figure 8-5. Passing on a different value than the received value—distorted.

3. Accepted and assimilated by an agent before being passed on to a third party with assurances of integrity (see Figure 8-6).

Figure 8-6. Passing on a different value than the received value—distorted.

Agent 2 now uses the data (value X) from Agent 1, and assimilates it as its own (X=Y). Agent 2 promises to pass on (conditionally upon receiving Y if X). It promises both involved parties to assimilate the knowledge. Only in this case does the knowledge of X become common knowledge if one continues to propagate this chain.

The first two situations are indistinguishable by the receiving agents. In the final case, the promises to make X=Y provide the information that guarantees consistency of knowledge throughout the scope of this pattern.

If we follow the approach promising integrity, we can begin to talk about engineering consensus of information, but not of knowledge. There remains nothing at all we can do to ensure that other agents will engage with information and become experts, other than forming a regular relationship with them to test their knowledge. This is Dunbar's price for knowledge.

Relativity of Information

Wrapping our heads around behaviours that happen in parallel, at multiple locations, and from different available views, is hard. In science, the analysis of this is called relativity theory, and many of the great minds of philosophy have struggled with versions of it, including Galileo, Einstein, and Kripke. The problem is no easier in information technology, but in the increasingly distributed modern world systems we have to do it all the time.

In database science, the so-called CAP (consistency, availability, and partitions) conjecture was a trigger that unleashed a public discussion about consistency of viewpoint in distributed systems—what Einstein called simultaneity, and what databasers call distributed consistency.

Most stories about simultaneity generally end up with the same answer: that simultaneity is not a helpful concept because multiple agents, players, and actors are doomed and sometimes encouraged to see the world from unique perspectives. Promise Theory helps to remind us that, ultimately, it is the responsibility of each observer of the world to find his own sense of consistency from his own perspective.

Promising Consistency Across Multiple Agents and CAP

Agents are caches for their own knowledge and for information that comes from outside. We've discussed how information propagates, but there is the question of who knows, and when.

Because there is value in consistency and expectation—for example, for reputation—many businesses and goods and service providers would like to be able to promise consistency across all of their service points, but it should be clear by now that this does not make sense. To begin with, we have made it a rule that one should not try to make a promise on behalf of any agent other than oneself, so promising for all agents is a stretch. Now let's see why.

A conjecture, commonly known as the CAP conjecture, was made at the end of the 1990s about how certain trade-offs must be made about a user's expectations of consistency and availability of information in databases. Although it was only about databases, it applies to any case where information is disseminated to multiple locations, which means always. Understanding the details goes beyond the scope of this book, but we can get an idea of the challenges.

The simple observation was that hoping for a perfect world with global and consistent viewpoints on knowledge was subject to certain limitations, especially if the parts of that world were distributed in a network with potentially unreliable connectivity or cooperation. This much is indisputable. The letters CAP stand for:

- C: Consistency means freshness and uniformity of data at all locations (no one lags behind updates once they have been made somewhere within the system; there is only one value for each key globally).
- A: Availability of the data service (we can access data in a reasonable time).
- P: Partition tolerance, a slightly odd name meaning that if we break up the system into pieces that can't communicate, it should continue to work "correctly."

Without getting too technical, let's try to see if we can define C, A, and P somewhat better, taking into account time and space, and using promises.

To make a Promise Theory model of data availability, we need to include all the agents that play a role in accessing data. Recall the discussion of the client-server model:

- C: A client who will make a request for data/state and give up waiting for a response after a maximum time interval. This limit is the policy that distinguishes available from unavailable.
- S: A server that will answer that request at a time of its choosing.
- N: The network that promises to transport the data in between, at a time and rate of its choosing.
- O: An observer to whom the answer would be reported by the client (as a final arbiter).

Each of these agents can only make promises about its own behaviour. A server agent can be said to be available to a client agent if the client receives a reply to its request from the server within a finite amount of time.

A Is for Availability

In accordance with Promise Theory, the definition of availability to the client is purely from the observable viewpoint of the client agent, and makes no assumptions about what happens anywhere else. The client takes the promises made by other agents under advisement and makes its own promises to obtain data conditionally on the assumption that they will try to keep their promises.

A definition of availability has to refer to time, as a time-out is the only way to resolve whether a reply has been received or not, without waiting forever. At what point do we stop waiting to know the answer? The client must have some kind of internal clock to make this assessment, else we have no way of measuring availability.

I added an observer as a separate agent to a client aggregator in Figure 8-7 to show the possibility of caching information from the server locally at any client. The observer might perceive cached data as live data and consider it (the cached data) to be available, because it receives a response quickly. Of course, now we have to worry about whether the cache is consistent with the value of the remote data.

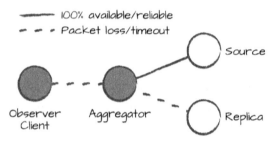

Figure 8-7. Availability of all or part of the data, or agents. Can we get the answers we need from some agent? What goes missing affects what we can say about consistency.

We see easily that availability and consistency need each other in different ways at different places and times — it does not makes sense to talk about the availability of the whole system, but only of the agents individually.

Availability of the server is needed to establish consistency of data at the client, and availability of the client has to be voluntarily curtailed to guarantee that the observer cannot see inconsistent values between the cache and data retrieved from the server (but how would an agent know?). See Figure 8-8.

According to the rules of Promise Theory, we would model the smallest part of the system that can change independently as a separate agent that makes individual promises (see Figure 8-8). Thus, for a database, this tells us that the availability promise applies to each data value represented here by the server independently, not the whole database interface, represented by the client.

Promise Theory tells us to lock, or limit, availability to data individually. We just rediscovered database transaction locking.

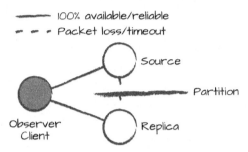

Figure 8-8. A partition between different sources means they can't equilibrate, back up, or secure data redundancy. An observer can still reach data, but if some systems suddenly failed, the versions might be out of sync. The user might even be able to see two different versions of the data. How would it choose?

C Is for Consistency

Consistency means that if information is recorded as having some value at some global time T, by any agent in a distributed system, then at any time following this, all agents should see that value (see Figure 8-9).

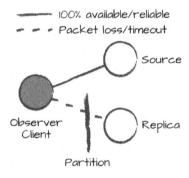

Figure 8-9. Partition on external availability (can't get complete access to data), but the part we see can still be self-consistent.

Notice that for keeping this promise, any agent needs to agree about the global time at which changes occur on another agent (i.e., they need to be able to agree about arbitrary points in time, or effectively have a common clock). This adds a difficulty, as global clocks don't really exist, for the same reason we can't have consistency of anything else.

If there is a single server, as in the availability discussion above, this seems easy. The server promises to provide the latest value. Then consistency is trivially achieved. But now, suppose that we have several users looking at the same information, but with different transit latencies. Suddenly, information is propagated to different locations at different rates, and the global view is lost. No agent can promise how quickly another can obtain it.

Global time does not help us at all because the finite speed of information transfer leads to inevitable delays. We cannot make promises once data has left an agent. In other words, no one can compare their results at any theoretical same time. At best, they could agree to compare results averaged over a coarse grain of time, or a time interval "bucket." That time interval would need enough slack for information to equilibrate around the system (i.e., travel from one end of the system to the other and back).

Banks use this approach deliberately when they cease trading at the end of each day and force customers to wait, say, three working days for transaction verification, in spite of modern communications. In some circumstances, one might place this determinism ahead of accuracy of timing, but there is a trade-off here, too. However we choose to define consistency, we have to deal with distortion of the history of data, an artificial slowdown in capture performance, or both.

To regain a global view, we can, of course, wait again until all the parts catch up. This is equilibration. To reach equilibrium, all agents in a system may promise to coordinate and agree on the same data values. In other words, the best promise we can make is: if you wait a number of seconds, I promise the data can be uniform, assuming that all agents honoured their promises to block further changes. In this sense, all consistency has to be eventual in the sense that a delay must be introduced somewhere.

To summarize:

- Consistency does not happen by itself, because the finite speed of information makes different values current at different times and places.

- Data values must come to equilibrium by cross-checking the values at different locations.

- We have to deny access to the entire system until all values are trusted or verified to be the same. This requires users to choose an arbitrary boundary at which we stop caring.

- What is the entire system? Does it include the end users?

Once again, all of the responsibility of choice lies with the observer or consumer of promises.

P Is for Partition Tolerance

"P" is the vaguest of the properties in the CAP literature. The meaning of a partition is clear enough, but what is partition tolerance? What semantics shall we imbue to the term? Well, it refers to what agents promise to do in the event that they need to rely on information that is located in a different partition (i.e., someone they can't talk to). An agent may be said to be partition tolerant if it promises to deliver a correct response to a query within a maximum time limit, even if its response depends on information from another agent in a different partition.

Although this sounds very ad hoc, it is theoretically possible to define a correct response for chosen regions of a distributed system, for every conceivable scenario, as a piecewise function, and get agents to keep such promises. However, these are, of course, dependent on the definitions of C and A, and the work required to do this is not useful. Then the only useful thing we can say is that partition tolerance cannot be defined for push-based systems at all because there is no way to know whether equilibration happened.

The World Is My Database, I Shall Not Want

At first glance, everything is a database. The entire world around us is something that we read from and write to—we use and we alter. Even if we restrict attention to IT infrastructure, our networks, PCs, and mobile devices, we are all living users of a massively distributed data system. From the point of view of CAP, this is abstract enough to be true, but how do we draw insight from it?

We need predictable platforms on which to build society. Users of services and information have to know what they can expect. This means we need certain standards of conformity to be able to make use of the services that infrastructure provides. Infrastructure should also be ever present for the same reasons. This is two of the three CAP properties: Consistency, or standards of expectation, and Availability, or ready for use. For the third property, P, we need to talk about all possible system partitions, not just client-server interruptions.

Some partitions are intended, such as access controls, firewalls, user accounts, privacy barriers, government institutions, differentiation of organs in the body, and so on. Some are born of unreliability: faults, outages, crashes, cracks, earthquakes, and so on. How services continue to keep their promises to users, while dealing with each of these, gives us the P for partition tolerance.

Any system can be discussed in terms of the three axes of CAP, as long as we are careful not to think too literally. By working through these ideas and the promises they make, we can design systems that meet our expectations. This brings us to the final topic: how to understand systems.

We need to get used to the idea of *many worlds* and only *local consistency* as we head into the future of information systems. As distances become greater and timescales get shorter, the ability to promise consensus between agents loses its meaning, and we're better off dealing with the inconsistencies rather than trying to make them disappear.

Some Exercises

1. If a chain of supermarkets promised a completely consistent inventory in all their stores, would you trust this promise? Why or why not? If a bank promises that your account balance will be known to all its branches around the world, would you trust this promise? If a restaurant promises that all members of a dinner party will receive the same meal, would you trust this?

2. Imagine arranging books, LPs, CDs, DVDs, and so on, on shelves in your home, so that they will be easy to find. Describe some possible ways of reducing this promise to specific properties of the books and the shelves.

   Is it possible to promise that it will be easy to find an item on the shelves? Suppose you group the books into categories. What promise can you associate with the pattern of placement? Consider whether the person searching for an item is a one-time visitor, or has a repeated relationship with the items.

3. A report about the crash of a passenger aircraft presents a narrative about a sequence of events, some of which happen in sequence, and some of which happen in parallel. The narrative discusses the promises made by technology, people, and incidental factors, such as the weather. What promises, or sequence of promises, can such a narrative keep?

9

Systemic Promises

A system is commonly understood to mean a number of parts that collectively perform a function by working together. Agents within systems have intentional behaviour, so they can make promises collectively, by cooperation, or individually. They can be built from humans, animals, machinery, businesses, or public sector organizations.

What Is a System?

A system is an emergent phenomenon. The virtual or systemic properties promised by a system come about from the collaboration of actual promises made by its internal agencies. No individual component within the system typically promises the qualities that a system embodies.

For example, the firefighting emergency service promises to cover half a city, respond to several simultaneous emergency calls, and put out fires within a maximum amount of time. There is no single component that leads to this promise being kept.[5]

Systems can promise things that individuals can't. If a military officer pointed to a soldier and shouted, "You, soldier, surround the enemy!" few individual soldiers would be able to respond. However, if the soldier was a superagent, composed of many collaborating parts (like a swarm of bees), it would be a different story. Systems may thus be strongly or weakly coupled collections of agents. A simple aggregation of residents in a building is not really a system, but, if all agents promise to work together, they could turn cohabitation into cooperation, and make new irreducible promises such as acting as a company.

---

5 The electricity company promises power continuously, without interruption. The police force promises public safety, but there is no public safety component.

The Myth of System and User

Systems are thought to be mighty, and users lowly (see Figure 9-1). More often than not we build the myth of system versus user, as a kind of David and Goliath story, because there is a *boundary of control*, or a region we call the system, in which we have a high degree of confidence in promises. Beyond this limit exist the users, like the savages beyond the city walls. Because we are not so close to them, they are treated differently. We are not sure about what promises they keep.

Figure 9-1. The separation of user and system is not inscribed in any Kafkaesque constitution.

The benefits of a system usually come about from the interaction between system and user, so why do we persist in this separation? One reason is that we use proxies to deliver the services by spawning off a surrogate of a system in the form of some kind of product that will be received by the user. At this point, the relationship between user and system becomes somewhat remote from the organization that built it. The surrogate does not typically learn or adapt as an active part in a cooperative relationship (though modern systems often allow upgrades, which are based on the learning of the parent system). Service industries have an easier time of this issue because they do not spawn off a surrogate, but rather continue in direct touch with their users.

The challenge in designing a system is to include users as a part of the system, and treat the promises that involve them just like any others within the machinery. The user is part of the machine.

The agency that is the final consumer is often not what we call the user at all. It is the agent that receives the outcome of what user plus system promise together. For example, a system might be a recording studio; the user, a band; the outcome, a musical recording; and the final recipient, the listener.

Systemic Promises

Let's think about what kinds of promises we expect from systems. At a low level, we might expect:

- Service levels and times (dynamics)
- Configurations or compositional chemistry (statics)

Two kinds of promises that belong to the system as a whole are:

- Engineered collaborative properties (aiming for direct causation)
- Emergent collaborative properties (emerging by indirect causation)

Some systems include users or clients, for whom desired outcomes are intended. We usually can't draw a clear boundary around a service part and a client/user part of a system; after all, they are connected by promises. Thus, the user must be viewed as a key part of the system, both through collaboration and outcome.

Properties that cannot easily be attributed to a specific individual include the following:

Continuity
> The observed constancy of promise-keeping, so that any agent using a promise would assess it to be kept at any time.

Stability
> The property that any small perturbations to the system (from dependencies or usage) will not cause its promises to break down catastrophically.

Resilience (opposite of fragility)
> Like stability, the property that usage will not significantly affect the promises made by an agent.

Redundancy
> The duplication of resources in such a way that there are no common dependencies between duplicates (i.e., so that the failure of one does not imply the failure of another).

Learning (sometimes called anti-fragility)
> The property of promising to alter any promise (in detail or in number) based on information observed about an agent's environment.

Adaptability
> The property of being reusable in different scenarios.

Plasticity
> The property of being able to change in response to outside pressure without breaking the system's promises.

Elasticity
> The ability to change in response to outside pressure and then return to the original condition without breaking the system's promises.

Scalability
> The property that the outcomes promised to any agent do not depend on the total number of agents in the system.

Integrity (rigidity)
> The property of being unaffected by external pressures.

Security
> The promise that all risks to the system have been analyzed and approved as a matter of policy.

Ease of use
>   The promise that a user will not have to expend much effort or cost to use
>   the service provided.

These are just a few of the properties that concern us. You can think of more desirable properties, or different names for these.

Although no particular agent could be blamed for enabling a property, it is plausible that a single agent could prevent the keeping of a promise. However, in systems, the chains of causation can be quite Byzantine. In fact, in any system of cooperative promises, there are loops that make direct causation a nontrivial issue. This is why it makes sense to think of systems as emergent phenomena.

A negative property like fragility seems like an odd thing to promise, but such a promise could be very important. We label boxes fragile for transport precisely to try to influence delivery agents to take extra care with them, or to reduce our own liability in case of an accident.

Who Intends Systemic Promises?

If no particular agent promises systemic behaviour, then who is responsible for the result? All agents and none are responsible. If that sounds like too much French philosophy, this is possibly because the whole idea of the system is abstract.

As always, Promise Theory's simple prediction is that it is not any part of a system that results in semantics. It is always the observer or recipient of promises that assesses whether or not promises are kept as intended. The assessment is in the eye of the beholder.

Thus any observer gets to make the judgement that a system is secure relative to its own knowledge. If we ask a consultant to tell us whether our system is secure, we'd better hope the he or she knows enough to predict every possible failure mode.

Suppose you want to promise *ease of use*. There is no *ease-of-use* plug-in or battery pack to provide this quality, so you have to look at the agencies you have and ask how could their promises result in the emergent effect of ease of use? Now you have to perform some semantic sleight of hand. Can you use already learned common knowledge or cultural norms to shortcut a lengthy learning process? Can you minimize the work required to learn an interaction pattern? At this point you might think, well if I'm going to impose something on these agents, why not just give commands? Why frame it as promises?

By now the answer should be clear. You could use impositions, but the agents might be neither willing nor able to act on them. They would not be as motivated to cooperate as if they were making voluntary promises that they saw an individual benefit in keeping. So, even if you propose promises for those agencies to keep, you have to put yourself in their situation, understand what they know and what skills they have, and then propose a promise. Would you make that promise in that situation? This is how to maximize the likelihood of a successful outcome.

Breaking Down the Systemic Promises for Real Agencies

Figuring out how systemic promises emerge from the real promises of individual agents is the task of the modern engineer. We should not make light of the challenge. System designers think more like town planners than bricklayers, and need to know how to think around corners, not merely in straight lines.

Directing birds of a feather to flock together as a systemic promise could involve arranging for individual agents to stay close to their neighbours. Another example might be that Godliness will result from promising to wash your hands often.

If you work entirely from the bottom up, you never have to confront the idea that some concrete agencies in your system actually have to promise real measurable outcomes, because it will happen automatically. It will be obvious. On the other hand, you might never confront the way users experience your system either. That means you won't understand how to build a lasting relationship with users.

The challenge of designing a system from the top down is that you never confront whether there are any agencies that can deliver appropriate promises. Your first thought will be to divide and conquer and you will start duplicating work.

Why Do Systems Succeed or Fail in Keeping Promises?

Systems of many parts promise a variety of attributes. A painting may promise form but not colour, or colour but not form. Does the painting collectively promise to represent its subject or not? Again, only the recipient of the promise can judge whether or not the promise has been kept.

Which part of a plane leads to flight? Which parts can fail without breaking the collective promise? There might be workarounds, like a skilled pilot gliding the plane.

A school might succeed in the promise of education:

- Because a specific teacher was helpful
- Because exams motivated students to study
- Because other students passed on information
- Because it had a good library

Only the individual student can say which of the promises, perhaps all, were sufficient in their own context.

Promises and intentionality come from humans, but humans keep promises through a variety of intermediaries, any of which might fail. When systems fail to keep promises, it might be unintended, or it might be deliberate deception. Much attention is given to the idea that failures are unintended and should not lead to the blame of individual humans or technological agents in systems. Very little attention is given to the notion of deception and deliberate sabotage of systems. It is common to point to individual component failures in computer malware, forged artwork, pirated music, and so on.

Dunbar's limitations can lead to systemic promise failures by overloading the capacity to maintain relationships. Packet loss and process starvation are the analogues in computing. As it is impossible to completely specify a human-machine system, and machines work on behalf of humans, it ends up being humans, not machines, who must make the system work.

Complexity, Separation, and Modularity

The matter of complexity in systems comes out a bit muddled in the literature. It has been suggested that it is the entwining or muddling of information that leads to complexity. This is actually quite wrong. Indeed, in a somewhat counter-intuitive sense, the opposite is true.

Complexity is measured by the explosion of possible outcomes that develop as a system evolves. This is a growth of information (also called entropy). When parts of a system interact strongly, it means that a change in one place leads to a change in another. This leads to brittleness and fragility rather than complexity. If you could replace 1,000 pennies with a 10 £ note, it would be less complex to deal with.

Sometimes fragility causes system states to split into several outcomes. Logical if-then-else reasoning is an example of one of those causes. It is these so-called *bifurcations* or branchings of outcomes that lead to the explosion of states and parts. This is provoked by strong coupling, but is not caused by it. Indeed, muddling things together reduces the total number of outcomes, so ironically it makes things less complex.

Separation of concerns (i.e., the tidying instinct), is in fact a strategy that brings about bifurcations, and hence proliferation. It leads to complexity because it increases the number of things that need to interact, leading to new entropy. Branching without pruning brings complexity. One of the reasons we fear complexity is because we fail to understand it.

The Collapse of Complex Systems

The separation of concerns is a very interesting belief system invented by humans. It has become almost ubiquitous in information technology and management. It is referred to as *siloing* in management. Promise Theory casts doubt on its validity.

One reason why belief in divide and conquer came about might be an artifice of our limited thinking capacities. Just as the limited size of an army leads you to deal with one invader at a time, so the Dunbar numbers for our thinking capacity imply limits on our brain power for handling other relationships. Similarly, our grammar skills do not support too many levels of parenthetic remarks, and we cannot do more than about five things at a time. All of these cases point to a strategy of trying to push away parts of a problem that we can avoid dealing with, similar to leaving behind travel items so you can actually carry your luggage.

The mistake we potentially make is in believing that our inability to carry the weight implies that the weight is not actually important, and should not be carried.

As a counterpoint to that idea, anthropologist Joseph Tainter made an interesting study of societies going back through time, looking for the reasons they collapsed. His conclusion was roughly this: as societies grow, there is a cost benefit to specializing into different roles to scale up. This is because individuals are not smart enough to be experts in everything; they have limited brain and muscle power. But that separation comes at a cost. If we want a service from a specialist, we now have to reconnect with them.

As agencies separate, they often form their own private languages that are not equilibrated with the general population, so there is a language barrier cost too. This leads to reduced trust. Agents then make clients jump through hoops to validate themselves. Bureaucracy and organizational silos are born!

Eventually, the cost of reconnecting through barriers (because of the loss of a trusting relationship) exceeds what agents can afford, and the system breaks apart as users begin to work around the barriers. Separation of concerns leads to collapse.

The autonomous agent model in Promise Theory makes this very plain. We centralize services in order to avoid the cost of talking to many other agents, but that puts all of the stress in one place. The bottleneck is born. The bottleneck then has to either limit its clients, or double up. As the service doubles up, a new service is required to coordinate the bottlenecks. The hierarchy is born. The hierarchy leads to further branching.

As the distance between agents increases, trust is lost and certainty demands adding more promises back to make up for the loss of the direct promises. The cost of all this infrastructure grows until agents no longer see a cost benefit to centralizing, and the structures break apart.

A goal for system design is surely to avoid this process if possible. The difficulty lies in evaluating which promises are cheap and which are expensive at any given time. It is the desire to save on costs that seduces us to reformulate these relationships and fall into the trap.

Through the Lens of Promises

What general lessons can we extract from thinking in promises? Promises are about:

- Formulating outcomes by destination rather than journey
- Which agents are responsible for the outcome
- How the constraints on those agents affect the ability to predict outcomes
- How access to different information affects each agent's view on whether an outcome was achieved

Instead of thinking of force or command, promises help us to see the world as a way to deal with constraints on the field of free possibility. Some observations that cropped up along the way:

- Client role: clients are responsible for obtaining service, not servers.
- Coupling strength is best kept weak to avoid fragility and dependency.

- Interchangeability and compatibility are about keeping intentions constant.

- In the end, it's all about knowledge, or what you know.

I've applied the idea of autonomous agents to both technology and to humans. Is that fair? Are humans really just agents? Of course, anything can be an agency for some observable effect. That is just how we label causation and understand the world. Humans, however, distinguish themselves by a more complex psychology than machines. (The psychology of machines is human psychology projected onto some kind of state machine.) As a human of some middling years, I have seen how aspects of human psychology intrude upon individual assessments and distort it in different ways.

Promise Theory pretends that communication and observation are relatively unambiguous, which is optimistic. If we intend to apply it to people, we'd better not get too excited about rational prediction. Human intentions and interpretations seem to be very noisy. Perhaps a warning would be in order on the package: "Caution: Promise Theory may cause headaches and tantrums if used together with humans." But this is true of all formal models.

Many themes could be tied up in a promise view of the world. More importantly, Promise Theory reveals, through simple principles, why individual subjectivity is important even in the relatively impartial world of engineering. It offers a few tools for thinking about the issues, and it even has some rules of thumb to avoid making the worst mistakes.

If you think in promises a little every day, I cannot promise that it will change the way you see the world (because that would violate your autonomy), but it might allow you to see things in sharper focus, and question the way we often impose assumptions on a situation.

You alone can promise to ask the right questions and take fewer promises for granted.

Index

About the Author

Mark Burgess is the founder, CTO, and principal author of CfEngine. For the past 20 years, he has led the way in the theory and practice of automation and policy-based management. In the 1990s he underlined the importance of idempotent, autonomous desired state management ("convergence"), and formalized cooperative systems in the 2000s ("Promise Theory"). He is the author of numerous books and papers on network and system administration and has won several prizes for his work.

Colophon

The cover font is Gotham. The text font is Scala Pro Regular; the heading font is Benton Sans; and the code font is Dalton Maag's Ubuntu Mono.

Get even more for your money.

Join the O'Reilly Community, and register the O'Reilly books you own. It's free, and you'll get:

- $4.99 ebook upgrade offer
- 40% upgrade offer on O'Reilly print books
- Membership discounts on books and events
- Free lifetime updates to ebooks and videos
- Multiple ebook formats, DRM FREE
- Participation in the O'Reilly community
- Newsletters
- Account management
- 100% Satisfaction Guarantee

Signing up is easy:

1. Go to: oreilly.com/go/register
2. Create an O'Reilly login.
3. Provide your address.
4. Register your books.

Note: English-language books only

To order books online:
oreilly.com/store

For questions about products or an order:
orders@oreilly.com

To sign up to get topic-specific email announcements and/or news about upcoming books, conferences, special offers, and new technologies:
elists@oreilly.com

For technical questions about book content:
booktech@oreilly.com

To submit new book proposals to our editors:
proposals@oreilly.com

O'Reilly books are available in multiple DRM-free ebook formats. For more information:
oreilly.com/ebooks

CPSIA information can be obtained at www.ICGtesting.com
Printed in the USA
BVOW06s0338160715

408953BV00030B/222/P